Growing Up Amish

A MEMOIR BY

IRA WAGLER

GROWING

UP

AMISH

Tyndale House Publishers, Inc.
Carol Stream, Illinois

Visit Tyndale's exciting website at www.tyndale.com.

Visit Ira's website at www.irawagler.com.

TYNDALE and Tyndale's quill logo are registered trademarks of Tyndale House Publishers, Inc.

Growing Up Amish: A Memoir

Designed by Jacqueline L. Nuñez

Edited by Susan Taylor

The author is represented by Chip MacGregor of MacGregor Literary, 2373 NW 185th Avenue, Suite 165, Hillsboro, OR 97124.

The names Sarah Miller, Sam Johnson, Gary Simmons, and, in chapters 17, 28, and 30, Eli, are pseudonyms, used to protect their owners' privacy.

Library of Congress Cataloging-in-Publication Data

Wagler, Ira.
   Growing up Amish : a memoir / Ira Wagler.
     p. cm.
   ISBN 978-1-4143-3936-8 (sc)
1. Wagler, Ira. 2. Ex-church members—Amish—Biography. I. Title.
   BX8143.W22A3 2011
   289.7092—dc22
   [B]   2011008109

Printed in the United States of America

17 16 15 14 13 12 11

7   6   5   4   3   2   1

This book is dedicated to my mother,
Ida Mae (Yoder) Wagler,
whose quiet inner strength sustained her through
the long and difficult journey that was her life.
She never wavered in her deep love for all her children,
even—and maybe especially—for her wayward sons,
who broke her heart again and again.
Her love was her sustaining strength.

ACKNOWLEDGMENTS

Special thanks to

Carol Traver of Tyndale, who made this book possible. You saw something, some spark in my jumbled mass of words, and took a chance when others took a pass.

My father, David L. Wagler. You pursued your dreams on your own terms and made them real, thereby lighting my path to my own dreams. In this effort, at least, I hope I did you proud.

My brothers and sisters, all ten of you. Your quiet support has been a rock to me through some of the darkest and most difficult times of my life. I love you all.

My fifty-nine nieces and nephews. You are my first and primary fan club, clamoring and contentious, but always intensely loyal and loving and supportive.

My old friends from way back, the original gang of six. Without you, there would have been a whole lot less to this book.

Marvin Yutzy. You are the best and truest friend any man could hope to have.

Those few friends, and you know who you are, who have been harassing me for the last fifteen years to write my story.

My agent, Chip MacGregor. You got my stuff to the right person.

Jerry S. Eicher. You freely shared with me your contacts in the publishing world.

Susan Taylor, my editor. You patiently and cheerfully took my raw draft of a manuscript and made it sparkle and flow. Along with all the other folks at Tyndale, you rock.

All my coworkers at Graber Supply, LLC. You were there beside me through so much pain and turmoil, until beauty was reborn from the ashes of my life.

LeRoy Whitman. When I was about to walk away and let it all slip through my hands, you called me back to my senses.

All you faithful readers of my blog. You created the foundation on which all the rest is built.

All those friends, too numerous to mention, whose lives touched my own in some profound way throughout the years.

PROLOGUE

ONE FATEFUL, STARLESS, APRIL NIGHT, I got up at 2:00 a.m. in the pitch black darkness, left a scribbled note under my pillow, and walked away—all my earthly belongings stuffed in a little black duffel bag.

Seventeen years old, bound for a vast new world. In my eager mind, the great shining vistas of distant horizons gleamed and beckoned. A world that would fulfill the deep yearning, the nebulous shifting dreams of a hungry, driven youth. And it would be mine, all of it, to pluck from the forbidden tree and taste and eat.

I could not know that night of the long hard road that stretched before me. That I was lost. I could not know of the years of turmoil, rage, and anguish that eventually would push me to the brink of madness and despair.

And so I walked on through the night. Within a month or so, all five of my buddies would follow. And the shattered little community of Bloomfield, Iowa, would reel and stagger from the bitter blow. From the shocking scandal, the shame and devastation of losing so many of its young sons to the "world."

My long journey had just begun.

PART 1

1

NO ONE SEEMS TO REMEMBER exactly what was going on at the old home farm that day. Can't say I blame them. There is no particular reason they should.

The one thing everybody does seem to agree on is that it was a typical late August day. Stiflingly oppressive heat. Barely a wisp of a breeze. Not a cloud in the sky. Not that I could confirm or deny any of it. I wasn't there. At least not when the day dawned.

Some of my older siblings claim the threshers were there— though it was awfully late in the season for threshing oats. The menfolk were probably clattering about in the barn loft, sweeping the old wooden granary bins where the oats would be stored. And soon enough, the neighbors would have come rattling in with teams and wagons to haul the bundled oat sheaves. The threshing machine would have been there too, pulled by an ancient hybrid of a tractor and set up by the barn before the first loaded wagons came swaying in from the fields. Sweating in the dust and heat, the men would have been pitching the bundles onto the conveyor belt that fed the belt-driven threshing machine, where they would have been chewed up, separated, and deposited into the barn as oats and straw. The late harvest was under way.

I'm guessing some of the younger kids were picking strawberries in the field out by the old hickory tree. Seems late in the year for strawberries, too, except for the Everbearing kind. Those plants produced from June until the fall frosts killed them. My father planted gobs of them every year to sell as produce—and to keep the children busy.

If Mom felt extra tired or stressed that morning, I'm sure she didn't let on. After breakfast, she and my older sisters were probably doing what they always did: washing dishes, cleaning the house, and preparing the noon meal for everyone, which on that day would include the threshing crew.

But then, my sisters remember Mom abruptly stopping what she was doing. Stumbling to a wooden chair by the kitchen table, her face twitching with sudden spasms of pain.

"Go fetch your father from the barn," she instructed Rosemary and Magdalena. And off they went.

"Mom said for you to come. Right away," they gasped. Dad dropped his shovel and rushed to the house, the girls tagging anxiously behind him.

Mom was sitting there at the table, white faced. "It's time," she told him. He turned and dashed off to the neighbors' place a quarter mile to the east. "English" people who had a car.

Moments later, my sisters stood silently by and watched as my mother—still sitting in her chair—was carried to the car by my father and one of the threshers. After easing the chair to the ground, Dad helped Mom shift into the backseat. Once everyone was situated—Dad, Mom, and the English neighbor—they headed off to the hospital in nearby Tillsonburg.

Except for Rosemary and Magdalena, I doubt the rest of my siblings had any clue what was going on. They may have noticed that Mom had gained some weight lately and that she seemed tired a lot. But in those days, in that setting, no one spoke of such things. Especially to young children.

Dad didn't return home until supper time, and when he did, Mom was not with him. My sisters remember the children gathering round.

"Where's Mom?"

"We have a little baby," Dad announced, beaming. "A boy."

They murmured excitedly. "A baby!"

"Mom is staying at the hospital tonight. We'll go get her tomorrow."

I'd like to think my birth was an important event, and to some extent, of course, it was. But in Amish families, the arrival of a new baby isn't treated the same as it is in English families, where everyone fusses rapturously. For the Amish, where it's not at all uncommon for families to have upwards of ten children, a new baby just isn't that big a deal.

By the time I came along, my parents already had eight children. Four boys and four girls. An even number of each. I broke the tie. Number nine.

I'd like to think, too, that the choosing of my name was the source of much somber thought and measured consideration. Serious weighing of various possibilities and combinations. Perhaps even reciting the finalists aloud a time or two, just to make sure the name would fit in the flow of all the others in the family.

I'd like to think it was an important ritual. But again, I know better.

Earlier that summer, Dad had hired a strapping young man to help with the farmwork for room and board and a couple of bucks a day. He was Dad's nephew and my cousin, probably around twenty years old. He was a fine, upstanding fellow, by all accounts. Hardworking, too. His name was Ira Stoll.

And by the time Dad had fetched Mom and me from the Tillsonburg hospital the next day, someone—I suspect it was my two oldest sisters—had come up with the fateful suggestion: "Why don't we name the new baby boy Ira?"

"After our cousin?" I can imagine Dad stroking his long black beard thoughtfully.

Mom, resting in bed, did not protest. In fact, I'm guessing she was even a little relieved. And so it was settled, in the most lackadaisical manner imaginable. With zero fanfare or fuss, I was saddled forever with the name Ira.

No middle name.

Just Ira.

Ira Wagler.

And thus began my life in the Old Order Amish community of Aylmer, Ontario.

2

THE OLD ORDER AMISH are a pretty exclusive group. And there really aren't that many around. By latest official count, right at a quarter million worldwide. It just seems as if there are a lot more, because, well, the Amish are so different.

So visible.

So quaint and old fashioned.

And so ideal. At least from the outside.

It's not their fault that English society finds them endlessly fascinating. Mostly, they just prefer to be left alone.

A few defining factors must exist for one to be considered Old Order. First, and most critical, no cars. Horse and buggy only for local transportation. Second, no electricity. Not in the house or in the outbuildings. Third, no telephones in the house. Old Order Amish fiercely and jealously defend these boundaries.

Of course, there are a few other defining characteristics. All Old Order women wear long, flowing, home-sewn dresses and some sort of head covering with chin strings. The men wear homemade trousers with no belt loops and no zipper, just a large, four-buttoned, horizontal flap across the front. Barn-door pants, we called them. And all the men have beards. At least the married men do. A full beard is pretty much a universal requirement. But no mustache.

Which makes little sense, really. If it's biblical to grow a beard, one would think it's just as biblical to have a mustache. It's all naturally growing facial hair. But somewhere along the line, back during the Civil War, supposedly, the Amish decided that mustaches looked too militaristic. And since that time, the mustache has been strictly verboten.

Not that this issue hasn't been a cause of much dispute and dissension over the years. Always, it seems, some wild-eyed heretic somewhere is spouting Scripture and publishing bombastic little pamphlets arguing in favor of the mustache. Such arguments, however logical, have always been rejected by the powers that be, with the mighty hand of the church forcing the heretic to either repent or be expelled.

Other than the facial hair thing, there is wide variation and a lot of inordinate fussing within Amish circles. Some groups use only hooks and eyes on their clothes; others use buttons and snaps. Some pull motor-powered machinery with their horses; others refuse to use motors at all, not even small gasoline engines. Some groups allow little phone shacks at the end of the drive; others have phones only at their schoolhouses. Still others have no phones anywhere and must bother their English neighbors in an emergency.

Most Old Orders use buggies with steel-rimmed wheels, though a few allow rubber-covered rims. In most communities, the men wear suspenders, or "galluses," to hold up their pants, but no communities allow belts. The size and shape of the women's head coverings vary greatly from region to region. As do the length and fit of their dresses. And so on and on.

Most Old Orders today have running water in their houses; only the plainest groups reject indoor plumbing. And some practice strict shunning of former members, while others are more relaxed about those who leave.

Amish life is made up of a mishmash of confusing rules about what's allowed and what's forbidden. Most of them make little sense, especially to those on the outside. They don't have to, as long as they make sense to the Amish themselves. Which, I suppose, they do.

Despite the differences, almost all Amish are considered Old Order as long as they don't allow cars or electricity or phones in the house. I say almost all, because some groups, like the Swartzentruber Amish and the Nebraska Amish of Big Valley, Pennsylvania, reject the Old Order label. For them, Old Orders are too modern.

• • •

I grew up in Aylmer, an Old Order community located about thirty miles southeast of London, Ontario. As Amish communities go, it was considered middle of the road, or somewhat moderate in its rules.

The Aylmer community was founded in 1953, after a small exploratory group, which included my father, traveled by Greyhound bus from Piketon, Ohio, to the Aylmer area to scout for suitable land to settle. Why they ever wandered into southern Ontario remains a mystery, at least to me. But they did. And for some reason—perhaps on a whim—they got off the bus in Aylmer, walked into the office of a local real estate agent, and asked if he knew of any farms for sale in the area.

After regaining his composure at the sight of the gaggle of

plainly dressed, bearded men before him, he allowed they had come to the right place—and what do you know, it just so happened that he *did* know of a few farms for sale.

He squired them about the area for a few days. Was most gracious and attentive. Probably couldn't believe the good fortune that had dropped out of the sky. Imagine it—a hapless pack of wayward Amish people emerging from the Greyhound and asking to buy land. An agent's dream.

And the men were impressed. Their new buddy showed them several farms for sale, amazingly all within a two-mile range or so. They boarded the bus and returned to their families, singing the praises of this new land. In the following months, they returned and bought farms. The Aylmer Old Order Amish had arrived.

Most of the original Aylmer Amish settlers were young—in their thirties and forties—with young children. It was a rare and unusual thing back then to just up and move and establish a brand-new settlement, especially so far away, and in another country yet. A bold thing. Even a brazen thing. Who did they think they were?

But those concerns didn't faze them. They were idealists, with their own progressive beliefs and newfangled ideas of how one should live. They were determined that this new settlement would be different from all the others. More pure. They would not tolerate the sinful habits and customs common in the older, larger settlements: smoking, drinking, or "bed courtship" among their youth. And their youth wouldn't be allowed to "run around" wild, driving cars and partying. This they purposed firmly in their hearts. Dark and humorless, the men peered about suspiciously for the slightest hint of sin among them.

The Aylmer community considered itself an example for the lesser elements.

The perfect church.

The "shining city on a hill," from which would come noble directives about how people should live. These were particularly harsh toward communities that allowed tobacco use and/or bed courtship. And toward fathers who worked away from home instead of farming. There were proclamations about not spending money eating out in restaurants and about how children should be raised and disciplined.

In time, people came in droves to see the place for themselves, the perfect church, the place that issued such grave and noble proclamations. They came from all over: from the small communities dotted about in the various eastern and midwestern states. From Michigan. From northern and southern Indiana. New York. Wisconsin. From the hills of Holmes County, Ohio. And, yes, even from the blue-blooded enclaves of Lancaster County, Pennsylvania.

The visitors displayed a wide variety of dialects and dress. Daviess County people talked fast and sloppy, with many English words mixed in. Holmes County people conversed in a slow drawl, taking forever to get anything said. Even their English taxi drivers spoke Pennsylvania Dutch. And Lancaster, well, those people used old German words we had never heard before and had no idea what they meant. We thought the Lancaster people the strangest. They were certainly the most unlike us. The men wore wide, flat-brimmed black hats, and the women sported funny little heart-shaped head coverings. We even heard rumors that their buggies were quite distinct from those in most other communities. Rectangular, like a box, with straight sides. Not angled in at the bottom, like those in most communities. And rounded tops. Hilarious to us, and strange.

Guests frequently arrived unannounced, often just minutes before mealtime. Many of my early childhood memories include having strangers in the house, company from other communities who stopped by for a meal or for a day or for the night. Mom always scratched together enough food for everyone. Cheerfully. Only later in life did I ever consider how inconvenient that must have been for her at times. My sisters, too, have commented how they would bake a cake or some other delicacy, only to see it wolfed down by hungry guests they would never see again.

Some guests left bigger impressions than others. Once, when I was about four years old, a couple stayed with us for the night. The man had salt-and-pepper hair, a sharp, pointy little beard, and piercing eyes. I was terrified of him for some reason and thought he looked quite evil. The next morning, as they were getting ready to leave, he looked right at me and asked if I wanted to go home with them. They needed another little boy, and I would be just the ticket. I was horrified and speechless, and wildly shook my head. He was, of course, only joking, but I didn't know that. I learned to keep my distance from our guests after that.

Once, several couples from Lancaster stopped by for a late afternoon meal. Only Dad and Mom ate with them. The visitors requested cold peach soup, which consisted of cold milk, peaches, and soggy lumps of bread. Standard fare in Lancaster County, we had heard. We lurked behind the curtains and watched as the adults sat there primly, visiting and eating the cold, gooey mess as if they enjoyed it. Though we were relieved not to have to eat the atrocious concoction, nobody collapsed after eating it, so it must have been okay.

Occasionally single men would make the pilgrimage to Aylmer, emerging from the hills of who knows where, on a mission to find wives. Wild eyed and shock haired they came, sometimes lurking about the community for a week or two. None, as far as I know, were successful in their mission.

One such long-bearded youth stayed with us for a few days. The first day, he asked for a basin of water and towels; then he disappeared behind our large barn to "wash up." I don't know why he didn't just use our bathtub. They probably didn't allow indoor plumbing where he lived.

It was a good thing, I suppose, to be exposed to Amish people from other communities. It greatly broadened our experiences and our views, albeit still from inside the culture. Sure, we made fun of what we had not seen before and what we didn't understand. But we absorbed it too. And eventually we came to respect others who were different from us.

It's a strange but indisputable fact: Even among the Amish, other Amish seem odd.

3

FEW SIGHTS ARE CUTER THAN AMISH CHILDREN. Little girls dressed in their bonnets and tiny, perfect, caped dresses; boys in homemade pants, galluses, and straw hats. Miniature adults are what they look like.

I was one of them. Probably not quite as perfectly coifed as Lancaster Amish children, the ones you see in picture books. I was a bit more ragged. Barefoot, mostly, in summer. Snot nosed and dirty from playing around the farm and on the muddy banks of our pond.

The ninth Wagler child out of eleven, I grew up amid the clamor and bustle of ten siblings. Five brothers and five sisters, each with his or her own unique quirks and personalities.

Rosemary was the oldest. Born while Dad was away doing service as a conscientious objector to World War II, she barely knew him. In fact, when he did make his rare visits home, she was afraid of him. He tried to calm her, and once he picked her up and playfully tossed her in the air. As he caught her, she broke her arm. She screamed in pain and remained terrified of him for months after that.

Rosemary was seventeen when I was born, and I have only faint memories of her in our home. When I was four years old, she married Joseph Gascho, a stern, hard-core Amish man, and they moved to a farm about a mile north and west of ours.

Magdalena arrived two years after Rosemary. She was a sensitive, softhearted child who loved animals and could not bear to see anything or anyone suffer. Once, after some stray cats arrived at our farm, the boys threatened to shoot them. (We already had enough cats.) Maggie, determined to find them new homes, fashioned paper signs with the words "Please feed me" on them and taped them to the cats. Then she tenderly carried the cats in a box over the hill to the east and released them by the road and quickly dashed back home. Surely, she thought, someone would pick them up and care for them. Sadly, the cats could run faster than Maggie and were awaiting her at home when she arrived.

My brother Joseph came next, the firstborn son. I'm sure my father secretly sighed with relief when Joseph came along. Now there was a son to carry on the Wagler name. Tall and lithe with a ready smile, Joseph was an admired figure in my childhood. Of all my siblings, his temperament is closest to mine. Brooding, melancholy, intense, but outgoing and friendly, too. As a young teenager, he once overworked a team while tilling the fields. One of the horses collapsed and died from the heat. Joseph struggled with the guilt of that for months.

Naomi was tall and dark, and she could sing. As a child, she sang with Dad almost every evening, just the two of them. She nicknamed me "Bobby" when I was little. Where she came up with that name, I don't know. Didn't make a lot of sense, but it didn't have to. She was my older sister, and I loved her.

Jesse was shy and withdrawn and stuttered as a child. After the family moved to Aylmer, Jesse was befriended by the elderly English couple who lived on the farm just east of ours. Of all my brothers and sisters, he was their favorite. They called him Buster Brown. Jesse grew into a stocky, burly youth and left home before I was ten years old.

Rachel was vivacious and outgoing, always smiling or singing, or both. An outstanding cook, she tirelessly fed us all. She knew what was going on in and around the community, who was in trouble and why, who said what and where. Even today, if I need to contact someone from the distant past, someone I haven't seen for decades, I notify Rachel, and she always gets it done.

Stephen was the only one of my father's sons who could till the earth and make it produce. He worked hard and demanded the same efforts from us. He took the initiative while still a teenager and worked the home farm. Cleaned it up. Plowed and planted fields that had lain fallow for decades. A natural leader, he led his younger brothers on many an exciting foray. As an athlete, he was the most skilled hockey player in Aylmer Amish history.

Titus was my next-oldest brother and my friend. We got into many scrapes together. We played around our pond in the warm summer months, fashioned rafts out of old fence posts, and sailed the "great sea." We shared books and dreams. Collected stamps. And fussed and fought a good bit as well. The three of us—Stephen, Titus, and I—formed our own clique. We were known as the "three little boys."

I was just shy of three years old when my last sister was born. Rhoda displaced me as the baby. During our childhood days, she ran around outside with me, a tomboy to the core. Of all of us, she was the only one who could truly communicate with animals. Any animals—cats, horses, cows. She even tamed a Holstein steer and hitched it to a cart. Drove it around like a horse while the massive steer ambled along contentedly. Rhoda was the tenth child and once again evened out the boy/girl ratio at five each.

Nathan broke that tie for good. The last, the eleventh child, and the sixth son. He and Rhoda hung out together a lot, as I hung out with my older brothers. When Nathan was about a year old, he nearly died after he pulled a pot of boiling water from the kitchen stove onto his head. Suffering third-degree burns, he had a high fever and lingered between life and death for several days. My father, ever reluctant to go to a doctor, refused to take him to the hospital. Instead, my parents applied a homemade lard-and-dough poultice and wrapped the burns with gauze. Eventually Nathan recovered. The burns healed, but the scars still remain about his head and neck.

Me, I was a raggedy little boy with a mass of wild, uncontrollable, curly black hair and large, deep-set, brooding brown eyes. I was very softhearted and sensitive, more so than my brothers. And a bit shy. Not particularly manly traits in the earthy culture that had produced me.

Once I caught a young sparrow that was fluttering vainly against a windowpane in the barn. But instead of twisting its head from its body and throwing it to the lurking cats, as I'd seen my brothers and friends do countless times, I walked a few steps through the barn door to the open air and set it free.

I never told anyone.

As I would come to discover later in life, one shouldn't be condemned for simply craving freedom.

•   •   •

My parents, David L. Wagler and Ida Mae Yoder, like most of the families in Aylmer, came from southern Indiana. Both Mom and Dad were born into old, established families in Daviess County, at that time a forlorn, backward place on the road to nowhere. Well established, but just different. Daviess is looked down on, ever so slightly, by staid blue-blooded folks in settlements like those in Holmes County, Ohio, and Lancaster, Pennsylvania. Like Nazareth in the Bible, nothing good can come from Daviess. Not much, anyway. People don't actually say that out loud, at least not in my hearing. Blue bloods are way too polite for that. But I know they think it.

I'm pure Daviess County stock. About as undiluted as it gets.

Mom and Dad's history did not particularly interest me growing up. My parents were my parents. They were just always there and always had been. Immovable, like the sheer rock face of a mountain cliff. And as indestructible.

It is difficult to imagine my parents as infants or young children because, being Amish, the family had no pictures. But they were children. In a time before penicillin, when diseases and plagues stalked the earth and infant-mortality rates were staggeringly high. Either could easily have succumbed at birth, or certainly well before reaching adulthood.

They were normal children, I suppose. Intelligent. Inquiring. Both were among the youngest in their respective families, welcomed by clans of clamoring older siblings.

David Wagler was a little boy in homemade denims and galluses and tiny rumpled shirts, with coal-black curly hair. Ida Mae Yoder, a little girl who stood about shyly with hands clasped before her like a protective shield. Amply mothered by her older sisters.

At age six they went to school with their peers. Swinging their lunch pails, they trudged the dirt roads to the one-room, public country schoolhouse where they learned their letters and figures, and to read and write and cipher.

They graduated from elementary school after the eighth grade, but Dad hungered for more. More knowledge. More education.

So he was allowed to complete a mail-order course and receive his high school diploma, a rare and odd thing at the time. He was the only one among his peers who had the slightest inclination to do so. And he was the only one who did.

The years passed, and David and Ida Mae grew into young adulthood. Dad was a sturdy, handsome young man. And Mom developed into an astonishingly beautiful young woman. I take Dad's word on that. No photos of her from that time survive.

They married on February 3, 1942, when he was twenty-one and she was five months shy of her nineteenth birthday. From the start, Dad did not get on well with Mom's family. The Yoders were laid back, more relaxed about things like church rules, and they viewed my father with some suspicion. This man, who had stepped in and snatched one of their most beautiful eligible females, came from a long line of strident hard-liners. You were Amish, or you were nothing. In Amish society, the wife takes on the husband's identity, not vice versa. So the Yoders had reason to somberly reflect on what the future might hold for their daughter.

My father maintained an uneasy truce with Mom's extended family for about five years. Then a group broke away and left the Old Order. Founded a new church that allowed cars and electricity. And telephones in the house. Lured by the prospect of modern conveniences, my mother's parents and all but one of her siblings left and joined the new church. This deeply grieved and angered my father.

After an exploratory trip to Piketon, Ohio, where a small new Amish settlement was struggling to life, my father decided to move there. And so he bought a farm in Piketon, and within a few months, they sold their farm and many of their possessions and left Daviess. My mother was sad. And pregnant with her third daughter. But she had little, if anything, to say in the matter. She went along dutifully, as was befitting and expected of an Amish wife. From that day on, she was pretty much separated from her close family ties and her roots in Daviess County.

• • •

Our farm in Aylmer was located along the main drag, toward the eastern end of the settlement. It was a functioning farm, of course, with wagons and horse-drawn machinery parked here and there around the buildings and in the pasture. The barnyard was home to a herd of ragtag, mixed-breed draft and driving horses; twenty or so head of beef cattle; and a couple of cows that kept us supplied with fresh milk.

Dad usually had a few hogs around, and Mom kept a flock of chickens in a coop in the barn for fresh eggs. Tack on our collie dog and a half dozen wiry, half-wild mouser cats that were responsible for feeding themselves, and there you have it.

That was home.

Rambling and unkempt, but home.

Because Aylmer was somewhat progressive, we were allowed to have running water in the house. There was one lone bathroom, with a toilet and bathtub, and once a week, on Saturday night, each of us took a bath.

In winter, Mom cooked on a wood-burning stove in the kitchen. In summer, she used a kerosene stove. In the mid-1960s, Dad added a concrete-block wing to the south side of the house. A summer kitchen and washhouse, we called it. During summer months, we set up the large table and pretty much ate all our meals there.

Most mornings, all of us would sit around the table eating toast and eggs and Mom's homemade biscuits covered in dark, rich gravy. After the meal was finished, we would sit quietly as Dad took up the German Bible and read a passage of Scripture.

Then we would kneel while he prayed aloud one of the old High German prayers from the little black prayer book. It was always comforting and calming to hear Dad pray. Over the years, he developed a singsong rhythm in his delivery, a cadence that easily lulled a sleepy child into slumber. I can't remember any particular concept of who God was from those early years. Obviously, though, he was a force who could be addressed only by reading words from a little black book. Never informally.

After the five-minute prayer was over, we all scattered to our separate ways.

The children to school.

The older boys to work in the fields or the barn.

And Mom and the older girls to their cooking, canning, sewing, and seemingly endless stream of housework.

4

FROM THE OUTSIDE, it might seem that Amish kids must be bored. Nothing to do but work and play around the home and farm. No TV, no video games. No computers. Not even so much as a bicycle in most communities. Children have only their imaginations, homemade toys, and maybe a little red wagon. But I can't recall ever being bored.

We were always tackling some project—building dams across the little creek behind the barn after a hard rain, chasing some adventure in field and woods and pond. And working, of course. From about age three, each of us had our own chores to do.

With all that going on, we didn't have time to be bored, although there was one possible exception: church, where we had to sit, silent and still, on wooden, backless benches for what seemed like an eternity.

And it quite nearly was, because Amish church services are long affairs, usually lasting around three hours, sometimes longer.

Services are held in homes, a practice dating back to our Anabaptist roots during a time when the authorities actively hunted and prosecuted those they deemed heretics. In an effort to avoid unwanted attention, our forefathers were forced to hold church services secretly in their homes.

In Aylmer, it was always a big deal to host church at your house. Around eight thirty in the morning, buggies would begin to trickle in. After letting the women out at the house, the men would proceed to the barnyard to park their buggies. After unhitching the horses, they always spent time at the barn, standing around and visiting in somber, black-clad groups.

Eventually, the preachers would slowly amble toward the house, followed by the older men, then younger men, and so on, all the way down to the teenage boys. (Seating was ordered strictly by age. It was considered an insult to step ahead of someone even one day older than yourself.) After everyone was seated on the long benches, one of the married men started the first song.

Amish songs sound a lot like Gregorian chants, but they are absolutely unique in flavor and tone. Written in old Lutheran German, the tunes are mournful, slow, ponderous, mellow, beautiful, melancholy, swelling, and up to twenty minutes long.

Legend has it that these songs date back to the time when our nonresistant Anabaptist forebearers were persecuted and burned at the stake by authorities of the Catholic church. Tradition says that they sang hymns as they were led to the stake in the public square and as the fire crackled at their feet. As they sang—or so the story goes—the worldly bystanders would dance to the faster upbeat hymns, stopping only after the flames and heat had extinguished the song. To combat such blasphemy, our plucky ancestors developed tunes that were much slower—so slow that dancing would be impossible. I have never been able to verify that such dancing actually occurred. In fact, I seriously doubt that it did. But it made for fascinating legend, and I believed it for years.

Like the German hymns, the rest of Amish church services are slow and somber and measured throughout. And stiflingly boring for the kids.

After several hymns, and after the preachers returned from their Obrote conference, the first preacher would stand and deliver a "short" sermon, as in twenty to forty-five minutes long.

After the first sermon, we'd all kneel for prayer. Next, the deacon would stand and read a passage—usually a chapter—of Scripture.

This would be followed by the main sermon, which was delivered by the second preacher. The main sermon could last from one to two hours. Needless to say, long-winded preachers are unanimously unpopular with the children, and probably with the adults, too. Not because of content, necessarily, but because it's hard for children and adults alike to concentrate after three hours or more have passed.

The sermons mostly consisted of a mixture of Scripture, gospel, and Amish rules. We heard from earliest memory the old Bible stories, spoken in intimate detail. From Adam, through Abraham and the patriarchs, all the way to the life of Jesus. And his death on the cross. It was all there, and it was all preached. And yet, somehow, the preachers all managed to weave the story into some strange brew of Amish context, the Amish rules and Ordnung. We were convinced, as children, that the Amish way was the only right way, the only true way. And that all those who were not Amish probably would not make it to heaven. Not that such a message was explicitly preached. But messages were preached in such a way that we could reach only that one stark conclusion. At least back then, that's how it was.

Aylmer had the normal contingent of three preachers: Peter Yoder, the bishop; Nicholas (Nicky) Stoltzfus; and Jacob (Jake) Eicher.

Nicky Stoltzfus was my least favorite. A tall, gaunt man with a long, majestic beard that curled out at the tip, well below his chest, he had hollow eyes hidden under bushy brows. The real theologian of the three, he preached by far the deepest sermons.

Barefoot he stood, preaching in a bone-dry voice.

Paying little heed to the time.

As a child napping with my head on my father's lap, I often wished Nicky would just shut it down and sit down.

I liked it much better when Jake Eicher preached. A fiery man with flat, straight-hanging hair and a bushy beard, Jake preached in a powerful, high-strung voice that invaded the last crevice in the remotest corner of the largest house. I've heard it said of Jake, perhaps unkindly, that he had one good sermon in him and we heard it many times. Probably true. But the man could keep the children awake and alert. He was my favorite, and the favorite of most children. We never napped when he rose to take the floor.

After the main preacher finally wound down, there was another long prayer—more kneeling. And finally, one last song, which could go on for another agonizing ten minutes or so.

Then—and only then—was church finally over.

I don't remember learning very much in church, mostly just wishing that it were over. Truth be told, the greatest lesson I ever learned in church actually came from my sisters.

One Sunday morning when church was at Alva Eicher's place, a family of strangers—probably relatives of somebody or other—had come in for the service. The father was really slick and cleaned up. Even his beard was trimmed. I heard later that they were from Nappanee, Indiana.

As we tied up the horses and prepared to go into the house, I noticed a couple of young boys hovering close to the slicked-up man from Nappanee. One of the boys was about my age and inordinately rotund. I stared at him, fascinated. His body was almost as round as it was tall.

All throughout the service, I watched this family, still marveling at this boy's size. I'd never seen anyone so young quite so large. When church finally ended and the children were released, we all excitedly rushed out to play.

Somewhere in the course of our play that afternoon, I approached the little boy. Round cheeked, he wore glasses perched on his pudgy nose. We stood there, sizing each other up. Hands in pants pockets. Awkwardly scuffing the dirt with our bare feet. At least, I was barefoot. He probably wore shoes, coming from Nappanee and all.

We stood there, face-to-face. I was on my home turf. He was a stranger in a strange land. He smiled hesitantly.

"What's your name?" I asked.

"Ernest," he said shyly. He smiled again, almost pleadingly.

Ernest. Never heard of a name like that before. I looked him up and down. Then into his eyes. "You are fat," I said. Flatly. Matter-of-factly. Little rancor involved.

His face fell. The smile vanished. His eyes widened with dismay and pain. He seemed to shrink into himself. Without a word, he turned and lumbered away.

I walked off. Didn't really think anything more about it. I didn't despise him. Or laugh at him. He was just different. He was, well, fat.

That afternoon, after we had returned home, my sisters talked of the strangers from Nappanee. And of the little boy. Ernest.

"Did you play with him?" one of them asked. Probably Maggie. She was always admonishing us to be nice.

"A little," I answered innocently. "He was fat."

Maggie looked sharply at me, startled and suspicious.

Utterly unaware of the effect my words would have, I blithely prattled on. "He was fat. I told him he was fat." It was a huge mistake.

My three sisters reacted with expressions of great horror and disbelief.

"You did *what?*" they shrieked, practically in unison. And right there, on the spot, an impromptu school session was called to order.

Three screeching teachers. One poor, unwilling little four-year-old student.

The tumultuous clamor of their voices echoed through the house in loud, overwhelming waves. I wished they would stop before they woke Dad from his nap. That wouldn't be good for anyone. I stood there, perplexed. I honestly wasn't sure what all the fuss was about.

"You can't do that, make fun of someone because of how he looks," Naomi lectured sternly. "It's not kind."

Kind? What did that have to do with anything? Truth was truth. Unwilling to concede without making a defense, I bristled.

"But he *was* fat," I said stoutly.

Alas, my rock-solid reasoning was promptly smashed and swept aside like so much dust. My retort triggered a cascade of even more anguished screeching. Many ominous scenarios were trotted out. What if people made fun of the way *you* look? laughed at your curly hair? How would you like that?

Although failing to see any connection between my hair and my apparently unforgivable sin, I nonetheless made a hasty tactical decision to not say anything more.

Shut up and retreat.

The screeching eventually subsided. Soundly admonished and feeling very chastised, I was released at last. Relieved, I dashed off to play.

My sisters' lecturing must have sunk in somewhat. I'm sure I committed countless childish transgressions in the ensuing years. But none even remotely approached the level of my stark, pure cruelty to a poor, overweight boy named Ernest on a long-ago summer Sunday afternoon in Aylmer.

5

I WANTED TO GO.

I *yearned* to go.

But I was too little, they said. And too young.

"Wait a few years. Your time will come soon enough."

And so, I watched my brothers leave, one at a time.

Each morning they walked out of the house, swinging their lunch pails beside them. They returned each afternoon around three thirty and told me about their day—all the things they had seen and learned. And of the books they'd read.

"When you turn six," my mother told me. "Then you can go."

Days passed.

Then weeks.

Then months.

And then one August, the big day arrived—my sixth birthday. Now I was old enough. And big enough. Finally, I could go to school.

I'll never forget my first day. I left the house with my brothers and trudged importantly down the road, clutching my pencils and a ruler. Swinging my new blue-green lunch box, I strode bravely up the cracked and ancient concrete walkway and up the steps into the big white schoolhouse.

Many of my classmates had already arrived and were milling about. Harold Stoll. Jerry Eicher. Willis Stoll. Abraham Marner. Lydia Wagler (my first cousin). And Lois Gascho.

We stood around, wide eyed in awe. A few looked as if they might cry. The second and third graders marched about, casting condescending glances at the little first-grade rookies.

I both liked and feared our teacher, Miss Eicher. Like most teachers, she had her favorites. I wasn't one of them.

I did have some small advantages, though. I knew my ABCs. I'd learned them at home from my older siblings. I could already read a bit from the tattered remnants of Dick and Jane books we had at home. And I could count in blocks of ten.

I quickly fell into the routine at school.

We learned to print the letters of the alphabet on rough paper in uneven, heavily pressed pencil lines. We learned to count and write numbers, and to add and subtract. And we learned to speak English. That was the rule. Only English at school. No Pennsylvania Dutch. After a few months, we were all moderately fluent in the language.

On the whole, I really liked school, although I could never admit it.

Girls liked school.

Boys weren't supposed to.

When asked by an adult, I scoffed and claimed I didn't. But I did.

The first year passed, and before long, I was one of the second graders. Now I could strut about with my classmates and look pityingly on the poor, confused little first graders, huddled in groups looking as if they might cry.

Miss Eicher was my second-grade teacher too. And no, I still wasn't one of her favorites.

I loved books and spent hours absorbing great chunks of words, to the detriment of my other studies. During that year, my class learned penmanship, writing in script. I hated it passionately. Our usual lesson consisted of writing sentences—usually about ten or twenty—from our lesson book. When we were done, Miss Eicher allowed us to go outside and play, even though it wasn't recess.

My friends Jerry and Harold zipped through their writing exercises, scrawling their sentences in mere minutes before rushing outside, while I sat at my desk, laboring mightily to finish my writing so I could join them. It took me forever.

Eventually, my frustration got the best of me. One fateful day, I scrawled a few illegible lines across the barren expanse of notebook paper and rushed outside to join my classmates. Miss Eicher usually didn't check our writing assignments anyway.

In our next writing class, I did it again. And again, in the writing class after that. And again and again.

I got away with it for weeks. It was my little secret.

But the day of reckoning approached.

Then it arrived.

I was heading in from outside after the first bell rang when I heard someone call my name. Miss Eicher wanted to see me at my desk. Right now.

A tremor of fear sliced through me.

I walked inside with a sinking heart. Miss Eicher was sitting at my desk, looking down at my writing notebook, a crowd of my classmates clustered around her. A low murmur drifted through the group. I caught snatches, whispers. *"A-a-ah." "O-o-oh." "Didn't do his writing." "Just made scribbles." "Teacher just caught it. . . ."*

As I walked the gauntlet, my classmates lined the aisle, staring with wide accusing eyes and jostling for a better view of the imminent inquisition. I sensed no pity in them. Only morbid fascination.

I approached my desk, feet dragging, and stood with a hanging head before my judge. She looked at me sternly.

"What's the meaning of this?" she demanded, motioning to the notebook spread open on my desk. The damning scribbles seemed to leap from the pages, screaming accusations at me before all the world.

I stood mute and wide eyed. I'd get a whipping now for sure. Miss Eicher had her established methods for dealing with miscreants. The prisoner would be escorted outside to the woodshed and left there to ponder his or her fate while Miss Eicher came back into the classroom, slid open a desk drawer, pulled out a sturdy wooden ruler, and marched back to the woodshed, where swift and severe punishment would be administered.

I had seen it. I had heard it. It had happened to my friends. Now my time had come, I knew. I swallowed, my brown eyes brimming with tears. But I didn't cry.

I feared Mom would find out. Oh, the shame. And Dad. Another whipping would follow at home. The seconds crawled by. Miss Eicher did not soften her stern, unrelenting gaze.

Abruptly, she instructed my classmates to fetch their writing books so she could check their work. Jerry and Harold, the two swiftest writers, scrambled piously to comply. They gleefully showed her all their finished lessons. They cast scornful glances at me. They wouldn't dream of doing what I had done.

I stood hunched and silent, guilty before them all.

Then Miss Eicher abruptly got up, rang the second bell, and afternoon classes resumed.

That was it.

She did not spank me, or even tell my parents (as far as I knew). But she did make me stay inside at recess and during lunch hour and finish every single abominable writing exercise I had avoided.

It took several days.

After I had laboriously completed the last dreadful assignment, she released me to join my classmates, and I ran outside gratefully.

It was never mentioned again.

Nor was it forgotten.

While I might have struggled with the tediousness of writing drills, it was the bigger questions in life that really held my attention—even at such a young age.

Twice a month, on Friday afternoons, we had art class, which consisted of the students' drawing simple things like birds and a sun with cascading beams in the upper corner and short slogans like "God Is Love" or "Love" at the bottom.

One day at recess my friends Willis, Jerry, and Philip and I stood examining the art displayed on the wall and trying to guess who drew what. One drawing had the usual "Love" slogan at the bottom.

We stood there with our hands in our barn-door pants pockets, or with thumbs hooked on our galluses—as we'd seen our fathers do at church—and discussed whether we really should love everyone. Even our enemies.

We agreed we should.

"But what about Satan?" Philip asked. "Should we love him, too?"

We respected Philip. He was a year older and a grade above us. Next year he would graduate to the west school where the big students went.

It was a startling thought. We grappled with the disturbing concept. Satan was wicked; that we knew from countless sermons.

He'd tempted Eve in the Garden and even now lurked about trying to get little children to do bad things.

But weren't we supposed to love everyone? Even him? We could not imagine that we should hate anything or anyone.

"Satan is bad. We shouldn't love him," I said tentatively. But I was unsure of my words.

In the next few minutes, the four of us hashed it out with serious observations and solemn comments, balancing the sin of loving evil against the sin of not loving at all.

We finally reached a consensus and agreed that perhaps we were obligated to love Satan just a little bit. Not much. Just enough so we wouldn't hate him, because hating was wrong.

Satisfied, we disbanded as the bell rang and returned to our desks.

We told no one of our conclusion. But I pondered the issue in my heart for months.

6

Soon after school began came the first frosts of fall.

As autumn descended on the farm, row upon row of whispering green cornstalks faded slowly to a greenish brown. Neighbors gathered and helped one another as teams and wagons plodded through the fields and returned laden with long, heavy bundles of cornstalks flowing over the sides and dragging on the ground.

The corn bundles were then thrown into the ravenous chopper, where they were shredded to bits before being propelled up the long pipes into the silo until it was bulging to the brim. The air reeked with the wet, pungent odor of fresh chopped cornstalks.

And every year Mom warned us all with terrifying tales of the awful things that could happen if one didn't respect the chopper and got too close.

My personal favorite was the classic tale of the little four-year-old boy from somewhere, sometime, who disappeared one fall without a trace. Right at silo-filling time, of course. He had wandered too close and fallen in when they were filling the silo and the chopper had devoured him. Nothing was seen of him again until the next winter, when they were throwing down silage to feed the cows. They found his chopped-up remains, in tiny bits, mixed in with the silage. We listened, wide eyed and appalled. I don't know if the story was actually true.

We all watched ourselves around the chopper nevertheless. No sense becoming a cautionary tale for future generations.

• • •

In the fall of 1970, I entered the fourth grade at the west school, where the big children went. I looked forward to joining the upper grades and proudly trudged off with my brother Titus. From the first day, things did not go so well.

Back at the east school, I was a big fish in a little pond. A tough third grader—a leader. But in fourth grade I was a tiny tadpole in a vast ocean. A nobody. A scrawny little kid to be kicked around.

And kicked around I was. But I deserved it. I didn't know my place. My big mouth was part of the problem. That, and my stubborn nature, which I had inherited from my father.

I wouldn't give in, but instead, fought my tormentors. Of course, I was instantly overwhelmed every time. It was pretty bad. One evening on the way home from school, a big eighth grader sat me down in a mud puddle on the road because I refused to retract a derogatory taunt I had foolishly hurled at him.

I wouldn't call them bullies, necessarily, the guys who tormented me. To them, I was just a smart-aleck kid who needed to be shown his place in the order of things.

Still, that fourth-grade year was the worst of my eight years at Amish schools. I hated it with a passion.

But it could have been worse. A lot worse, for a lot longer. As it was for another Aylmer Amish boy: Nicholas Herrfort.

Almost every Amish community has that unusual, or odd, family, as do most English communities, I suspect. They dress differently. Talk differently. Act differently. In Aylmer, that family was the Herrforts.

Solomon Herrfort had moved to Aylmer as a single man. He emerged from the backwater area of the plain and very conservative Milverton, Ontario, community. He worked for a time as a hired hand for my uncle, Bishop Peter Yoder. Later, he married Esther Gascho, and they settled on a small farm a few miles northwest of our home.

Solomon was different, no question about it. He was small, lean, and wiry, with a shock of unruly orange hair and a stringy, dirty-orange beard. He was a bit slow and eccentric and hard of hearing. His typical response to any comment was a prolonged "Ooohhh," probably because he couldn't hear what was said to him. We children made fun of him and said he had wax in his ears.

A grove of tall trees obscured the dull brick house on his farm at all times, even on the sunniest day. The house itself was spooky, with many sharply peaked gables. It was always gloomy after dark; the only light was the pale, flickering glow of the dismal little kerosene flame lamps the family used in their home.

The Herrforts never took a turn holding church services in their home like other families, and they rarely socialized with other families in the evenings. Solomon didn't like to be on the road with horse and buggy after dark. The family was as close to reclusive as any I've ever known.

They were also poor. Really poor. What Solomon did for a living remains a mystery to me. I suppose he farmed a bit and had some goats. I don't know what the family ate. Whatever it was, it wasn't much, and it probably wasn't healthy.

Esther was always frail and in poor health and could never seem to get her housework done. My sisters recall being sent over to help Esther clean her house. The Aylmer families took turns, helping her out as needed. Every time a new baby was born to the Herrforts, the neighbors swarmed in and scrubbed the house top to bottom while Esther was at the hospital.

Solomon and Esther had six or seven children. They all wore ill-fitting, ill-made clothes, and they always looked thin, pale, and sickly.

Children of any age and in any culture are pitiless and cruel and run in packs. And heaven help the ones rejected by the pack. The Herrfort children were taunted and tormented as heartlessly as any I have ever witnessed.

Nicholas, the oldest, was born in 1963, sixteen months behind me. He always seemed much younger because he didn't start school until he was seven; almost all the children from other families started at age six. Nicholas was small for his age and always dressed in thin, shabby clothes and worn-out shoes some other family had given him. His front three teeth were missing, and he had a strange haircut. Straight across his forehead above the eyes, then straight back to the ears, then straight down over the ears. It was different. And we mocked and scorned him for it.

In fact, Nicholas Herrfort provided the perfect defenseless target for just about any kind of mockery—simply for the general merriment of the crowd.

"Are you a heifer?" the taunt would begin.

"No, no, Herrfort," poor Nicholas would respond.

Then again. "Are you a heifer?"

"No, no, *Herrfort.*"

The exchange would be repeated over and over to roars of appreciation and snickers of delight from sadistic onlookers.

Nicholas and his sister Nancy were always the last ones chosen for playground games. And neither of them could sing; their flat, toneless voices rang in jarring dissonance when it was their turn to lead a song. One time, Nancy picked a song that no one knew, and the whole classroom snickered and scoffed at her mistake until she buried her face in her arms on her desk.

I can't imagine what their existence was like, but the Herrfort children must have developed a dull numbness to the cruel horrors that constituted an average day in their threadbare and joyless lives.

Several bullies took a particularly twisted joy in making Nicholas's life miserable. They delighted in torturing and actually hurting him physically. The rest of us did not, but we did stand by and watch. We did nothing to stop it. And it was wrong of us, so very, very wrong. All of it.

The mocking.

The tricks.

The jokes.

The laughter.

The torment.

One particular thing still haunts me. I can see it as clearly in my mind as if it happened yesterday.

The school had an outdoor privy located across the yard from the schoolhouse. When Nicholas needed to go during the noon hour, he knew the bullies were keeping careful watch for him. Lurking furtively inside the safety of the schoolhouse, he waited for his chance to sprint to the privy without interference. When he thought the coast was clear, Nicholas would take off running down the walkway at full speed, legs churning desperately, arms pumping, hair flying behind him. But at least one of the bullies always raced after him. Once he caught up, he would kick Nicholas from behind with all his might, laughing and cackling all the while.

In winter, the bullies delighted in chasing him around to the back side of the schoolhouse, pelting him with iced snowballs and rubbing his face and hair with ice and snow, belittling and cursing him just for being who he was. It bruised him physically. It had to hurt, bad. I can't fathom what it did to him emotionally. And the rest of us did nothing to stop it.

Once, one bully egged on another student, younger and smaller than Nicholas, in the school basement. The younger student ran at Nicholas full speed, grabbed his long hair, and actually swung himself off the ground and around Nicholas. Nicholas stammered and staggered, crying, "Ouch, ouch, ouch." The bully whooped and clapped and guffawed and cheered. This happened two or three times, and again, we all stood around and watched until another student finally stepped in and stopped it.

The scene still sends shivers of horror down my spine. Especially because I knew better. Nicholas and his sister often walked home the same way we did, and on those walks, I quickly realized that they were both starved for even the tiniest crumb of human kindness. I can still see Nicholas as we walked along the road in the late afternoon sunlight, stammering his words, smiling hesitantly and shyly, and glancing furtively at me now and again to see if I would mock or scorn him. Gaining confidence when I didn't. We had many normal, lighthearted conversations. Laughing and chattering as children do. I suppose that was as close as I ever came to seeing the innocent, relaxed child he would have been in a safer, saner world.

It is no surprise that from the brutal foundation of such a tortured life, Nicholas developed a mental disorder as he grew older. While some of those mental problems likely were genetic, I am convinced that no normal child could have remained emotionally stable after enduring what Nicholas did growing up.

In 1994, the Herrfort family moved to Bland, Virginia. What

drew them there I do not know. It was a poor, remote community. Of Nicholas's life at this time, I have few details. Some say that after the move to Virginia, he stopped taking medication for his mental problems. Whatever the facts, I do know that his mental condition deteriorated steadily.

In June 1996, Nicholas's parents decided Nicholas would be better off living with relatives in Aylmer, as he was becoming a bit too much for the family to handle in Virginia.

Nicholas was vehemently opposed to the plan. He did not want to leave Virginia, but his parents insisted. At four thirty on the morning they planned to leave, Nicholas got up and left the house. After the sun rose, he was nowhere to be found.

His family searched and searched. And called and called his name. There was no answer. Sometime around midday, they found him. Lying facedown in a shallow pond just sixteen inches deep. He had taken his own life by drowning. By the time his body was found, the turtles had already eaten away part of his face.

No one can know the depths of his mother's raw and bitter sorrow for her oldest son, her firstborn. I do know, however, that I couldn't stop thinking about Nicholas and all that he had endured. Rather than being accepted and treated as an equal among his peers, he had been rejected and ridiculed simply for being different. My heart ached with regret, wondering how his life might have been different if just one of us had cared enough to be his friend.

They buried Nicholas in a remote country graveyard in Pearisburg, Virginia. A busload of relatives from Aylmer attended the funeral. A simple wooden marker was erected above his grave.

I thought about the shy, stammering, smiling boy who laughed and chattered as we walked along the road in the afternoon sunlight on the way home from school. And then I thought about the cruel injustices inflicted on him by those who should have known better and should have protected such a weak and defenseless child.

We knew who we were. And we know who we are today. We can mourn and grieve our thoughtless and cruel actions. We can say we were just children. We can say we didn't mean it. We can even ask forgiveness from the Herrfort family and from God.

But not from Nicholas. Not ever from Nicholas.

7

My father was a man of many gifts and skills.

Farming was not one of them.

He dutifully tilled the earth and planted the seeds each year, and they produced. But his heart was not in such work. And it showed about the farm. Fences in a state of semi-repair, rusting skeletal hulks of old junk machinery parked about, willy-nilly, in the field just south of the barn. We didn't realize it then, but our farm was just plain trashy.

That's not saying my father was a lazy man or that he didn't provide for his family. Far from it. Dad was a born salesman who loved the art of the deal. He sold nursery stock, fresh produce, and raised and sold purebred Landrace hogs.

Dad was also a gifted dowser, or "water witch"—although he stridently rejected that label. Dowsing has always had a bit of a shady reputation. During the Middle Ages, it was even believed to be from the devil.

It has never been scientifically proven to work, and most people today still view it with suspicion, fear, and skepticism. But growing up, I saw it with my own eyes, many times. If there was water to be found below the ground, not only could my dad locate it, but he could even tell you where to drill for the best flow and the clearest water. His record for accuracy was 100 percent.

Chuck Norman was the local well driller. He was known to everyone as simply "Fine and Dandy," because that was his automatic response to most questions. He used the phrase to answer anything from a question about how he was feeling to a comment about the weather.

Tall, wiry, and toothless, he was always dressed in stained olive-green coveralls and wore a dented, dirty, yellow hard hat, his ever-present cigarette dangling from his lips or cradled in a grease-blackened hand.

He usually showed up at our farm in the evening, after supper. Dad always walked out and greeted him. "How are you tonight?"

"Fine and dandy. Fine and dandy," he would reply, smiling his toothless grin and lighting another cigarette.

Dad would then walk out to a tree in the yard and break off a slim, Y-shaped branch. Then with one or two of us boys, he would pile into Fine and Dandy's dilapidated old pickup and we would roar down the gravel road to the place where Fine and Dandy was fixing to drill another well.

Dad would get out of the truck holding his little forked tree branch straight out in front of him, with his palms up and his thumbs out. He would then begin to walk slowly back and forth across the lot in the general area where Fine and Dandy wanted to dig a well.

It must have been quite the sight—an Amish man in a battered, wide-brimmed, black felt hat, holding a forked stick and slowly crisscrossing the yard, while a dirty, chain-smoking roughneck and a ragged little boy in galluses lounged off to the side watching.

Sooner or later, the branch in Dad's hands would lunge downward, quivering, as if alive and pulled by some invisible force.

"This is where you want to drill," Dad would announce, standing over the spot.

Fine and Dandy would smile his toothless smile, hand Dad a crumpled ten- or twenty-dollar bill, and take us home again in his dilapidated pickup.

Fine and Dandy always drilled exactly on the spot Dad had marked. Sometimes hundreds of feet down. And he always— *always*—found good wells with abundant supplies of fresh, clear water. Thanks to my dad, Fine and Dandy developed quite a reputation as a top-notch driller of wells that never ran dry.

I don't know where Dad's "gift" came from, and I don't know why he had it. Or how it worked. It may have been a latent ability, a remnant of ancient practices, buried deep within the psyche of his Swiss-German heritage. I don't think even he knew quite what it was or why he possessed it.

All he knew was that he had the gift and he could use it.

But when it came to passion and purpose, my father was committed to the one true calling of his heart. He wrote.

For decades he was a scribe for *The Budget*, a weekly newsletter for the Amish and Mennonites, and he developed quite a fan base. By the time I was born, he was already widely known throughout the vast majority of Amish and Mennonite communities in North America—and even overseas. But after he cofounded Pathway Publishers in the late sixties and launched the monthly magazine *Family Life*, his name became legend. Aylmer had been well known before, but after the launch of *Family Life*, it became something akin to a pilgrimage destination for Amish families from other communities.

Family Life was Dad's baby. His dream. His impossible vision. A magazine published by the Amish, for the Amish. To fund it, he mortgaged the farm (despite my mother's protests).

He must have seemed insane. Such a thing had never been attempted before. But he plodded determinedly forward. He placed ads for subscriptions in *The Budget*, formatted and published the inaugural issue, and then sent it out free to thousands of Amish households across the United States and Canada. Amazingly enough, it worked. Subscriptions poured in, eventually reaching thirty thousand.

Family Life was (and is) a very nice little magazine—if you like didactic stories in which the protagonist always repents after harboring heretical notions of leaving the Amish faith, or some such similar crisis. And the wayward son always returns in true humble repentance to court the plain but upstanding girl who is actually very beautiful inside, which, as we all know, is what really counts anyway. A glad light springs from her eyes as she modestly welcomes his return. Or maybe the glad light springs from his father's eyes. I can't remember. Whatever. The fiction was all pretty formulaic and predictable.

To be fair, *Family Life* also published a lot of useful, practical stuff—farm tips and such. Yet as unrealistic as a lot of the magazine's content was (and is), it was read with great gusto and satisfaction across a broad spectrum of Amishland.

Naturally, a pocket of hard-core, conservative Amish people resented and resisted my father's efforts. These people felt that one should read only the Bible. And maybe *The Budget*. Any other supplemental reading was deemed unnecessary and possibly sinful. Sad to say, those people still exist out there.

Regardless of the response, when I was growing up I could never admit my last name to any person even remotely connected to the Amish without being asked if I knew David Wagler. I always admitted reluctantly that, yes, I knew him. Not because I was ashamed or anything, but because it just got really old really fast.

The questions always continued: Are you related? Again, a grudging affirmative. More persistent and increasingly excited questions would invariably follow. Eventually the truth always emerged to rapturous exclamations of disbelief and accelerated heart palpitations. Seriously.

Once, in the mid-1980s, my brother Nathan and I were staying in Sarasota, Florida, for a few months over the winter, and an elderly Mennonite man from Arthur, Illinois, drilled us with the usual litany of questions until he finally got us to admit who we were. After our confession, he leaned on his tricycle in stunned silence for a few moments. He seemed drained.

I couldn't resist, so I said playfully, "Just think, now you can go back home and tell everyone you met David Wagler's sons."

He stood mute for another moment, still leaning faintly on his tricycle. I thought he might not have heard my comment. Then he quavered, "They probably wouldn't believe me anyway."

Today, my father is still well known in the Amish world, though his star is receding. The middle-aged to elderly speak of him, but the younger generations increasingly know him not.

Dad wrote steadily for many decades, producing many thousands of pages. Some of his stuff was good, some was okay, and some was, well, hard-core Amish polemics. Writing was his life's focus, and he neglected many other important things in pursuit of his passion—including, to a large extent, his wife and his children. That's not a judgment. It's just a fact.

He was a strong, driven man, and I deeply respect his accomplishments. But I wonder sometimes how far he could have gone had he not been hampered by Amish rules and restrictions. And whether he could have found a broader audience for his writings.

I have often tried to imagine what my father would have been like as a young man. Knowing him for the dreamer he is, I have wondered what he thought as he listened to his friends share local gossip and their meager dreams and humble goals.

Like me, I'm sure he was always painfully aware of how much more there was beyond the boundaries of his unsophisticated world.

Perhaps, lured by the modern conveniences of the surrounding society, he longed to drive one of the roaring roadsters that passed his plodding team and wagon in the heat, leaving him strangled and choking in swirling clouds of dust.

Perhaps, tempted by the throbbing dance music wafting from the pool hall in town, he allowed himself to briefly roam far and free from the mental chains that bound him.

Perhaps at times he questioned his roots and his background and the value of the traditions his elders clung to so tenaciously.

Perhaps he chafed at the narrow confines of the simple, unquestioning Amish theology that demanded his abject submission to an ageless tradition that taught any other path would lead to eternal damnation in the fires of hell.

Perhaps all these things and more occurred, calling to him, daring him to forsake forever the seemingly senseless traditions that confined him.

Perhaps.

But unlike me, in the end, he chose to stay.

8

ON THE OUTSIDE, Amish communities seem stuck in time, immune to change. But in reality, even places like Aylmer are in a constant state of flux. Nothing stays the same.

Events unfold. Below the surface, things are always happening. Disputes arise. Tensions flare. People come and go. By the time I was ten years old, some minor tremors had shaken the little community that was my world.

In 1968, my uncle Peter Stoll, a great jovial bear of a man and one of Aylmer's founding patriarchs, abruptly decided to leave and move to Honduras.

Honduras.

Halfway across the world.

His goal was to start a new Amish settlement there, help the natives live better lives by teaching them Amish farming methods, and gain converts. This was a strange and startling thing, coming from an Amish man. The Amish traditionally live their beliefs quietly and don't go around proselytizing a whole lot.

But Peter Stoll was different: softhearted and driven by a fervent desire to help the less fortunate. And once gripped by his vision, he didn't waste a lot of time tolerating second-guessers. In short order, he sold his farm, held a public auction to dispose of excess goods, and set off for Honduras, thousands of miles away.

A few other Aylmer families got caught up in Peter's vision and moved with him. Their departure really shook me up, especially because several of my classmates and good friends left with them.

Just like that.

Gone.

Out of the community, and out of my life.

There must have been something in the air around that time, because no sooner had the Honduras settlers left than our austere, barefoot preacher decided to scratch the itch that had been bothering him as well.

Long considered somewhat of a fringe element in Aylmer, Nicky Stoltzfus and his wife, Lucille, sold their farm and moved to a small, isolated community somewhere in the Midwest—someplace where they could live in extreme simplicity, where Nicky could allow the bristle of his mustache to sprout into the real thing, and where he could preach his long, bone-dry sermons in peace.

Even Bishop Peter Yoder got caught up in the moving frenzy. Shortly after Nicky and Lucille pulled up stakes, Peter and his wife, Martha, decided to leave Aylmer as well and join a new settlement that was starting up in Marshfield, Missouri. And once again, several other Aylmer families followed.

Why they went and what they were searching for was beyond the comprehension of my young mind. They just moved, and that was that.

Amish people do that once in a while, for reasons not readily apparent to little children.

But not our family.

We stayed put. My father's feet were firmly planted in Aylmer. He had no intention of moving anywhere, and that was fine by me. Aylmer was the only home I had ever known. I couldn't imagine living anywhere else.

Some of my older brothers and sisters, however, could.

● ● ●

My sister Maggie was the first to leave. Fed up with Aylmer's harsh rules and stifling discipline, she moved to Conneautville, a small town in northwestern Pennsylvania, where she took a job working in a nursing home. For a while, she attended services at the New Order Amish church in the area, but after a few years, she decided to leave the Amish altogether and joined a local Mennonite church.

When she informed my parents of her decision, they made a hasty trip to Pennsylvania to try to convince her to change her mind. Mom didn't say a whole lot. But Dad did. He blustered and cajoled and begged and threatened, but it was all in vain. Maggie remained firm.

Frustrated, Dad could do nothing, and they returned home defeated.

Those were tense and turbulent times. It was a huge blow to my father's ego to have a daughter up and leave the Amish like that. My father was among the leading intellectuals of his people. A writer of many great stories, all laced with moral lessons and conclusions. Not to mention a strident defender of the Amish faith and lifestyle. What would his readers think?

Of course, even as Maggie embraced her new life of freedom,

she still felt a connection to her roots, and returned home now and again to visit for a few days—truly a brave thing for her to do.

Dad always accosted her from the instant she walked in the door, berating and admonishing her incessantly during her entire visit. Frankly, I'm amazed she ever came back at all. But she did. And the other children were always delighted to see her.

Then it was Jesse's turn. At eighteen, Jesse was a strong, silent, burly young man—an intelligent loner who didn't say much but thought a lot. And somewhere, deep inside, he instinctively knew there was something more, a better life, somewhere out there.

Quietly, secretively, he made his plans. And then one night, without warning, he just slipped out through an upstairs window and disappeared.

He turned up a few days later in Cleveland, Ohio, where he was soon visited by Dad and a small but strident contingency of Aylmer preachers.

Jesse sat there silently as they cajoled, pleaded, and admonished.

Would he not just come home and try it again?

Surely it couldn't have been so bad.

It was all a misunderstanding.

Things would be better if he just came home.

Finally, against his better judgment, and after months of un-relenting pressure, Jesse allowed himself to be persuaded, and he returned home.

He tried to settle back into the flow of things, but it was no use. Dad's shimmering promises drifted off in the wind like the fluff they were. Things had not changed and would not change. Less than a year later, Jesse packed his stuff and walked out. This time his face was set. He would not return.

He lived for a few months in St. Thomas, about ten miles west of Aylmer. Eventually, he moved to Daviess County, Indiana, the area my parents had left decades before. There he connected with his Yoder relatives for the first time. They received him—a total stranger bound to them by blood—with great joy and open arms. He settled in, joined a Mennonite church, and built a stable, happy life. Eventually he married Lynda Stoll and moved to her home community in South Carolina.

Unlike Maggie, however, Jesse rarely returned to Aylmer and pretty much became a stranger to his younger brothers.

Naturally, my parents were shocked and stunned both times Jesse left. We all were. Mom broke down and wept as if her heart would break. It was a brutal thing, the thought of her child out there all alone in the cold, dark world.

Jesse was the first of her sons to pack a bag and simply walk away into the night.

He would not be the last.

• • •

The departure of Peter Yoder and Nicky Stoltzfus marked the end of an era in Aylmer. The old guard was gone. It was time for a new dawn.

And so two ordinations were held in Aylmer about a year apart. The first was that of Elmo Stoll. The second, Simon Wagler. They were both very young—in their upper twenties, maybe thirty—and were greatly burdened with their callings.

Of the two, Elmo Stoll rapidly rose to a position of prominence. Soon after his ordination, he finagled his way to a pinnacle of influence and unquestioned power such as Aylmer had never seen before and has not seen since.

Elmo had a grand vision of how things should be. He was a natural leader, a gifted man. A spellbinding speaker and preacher, he moved aggressively to solidify his power. He quickly overwhelmed and swept aside the kindly elder preacher, Jake, and

began to deliberately dismantle the structural safeguards that
Peter and Nicky had left behind.

A hard-core Amish firebrand, Elmo set out to please a furious, frowning God, a God who just might be placated if enough
sacrifices were made for his favors.

Suddenly, stricter rules were in place, and things that had always
been allowed in Aylmer were proclaimed sinful and forbidden.

Wire-rimmed glasses only, no more plastic frames.

Longer dresses.

Bigger head coverings for the women.

Buggy interiors painted black.

And the builders, the few that remained, were forbidden to
accept jobs that required any transportation other than a horse and
buggy, which greatly restricted their range and their livelihoods.

It was never enough, though. Elmo was restless and driven. He
never stopped tweaking the church rules and was always dreaming
up more stringent requirements.

At first, most people grumbled and complained a good bit.
But Elmo was a very persuasive speaker, and as he preached in
mellow, lilting tones, smoothly conveying his vision of how things
should be, members of the community began to see things as he
did—albeit begrudgingly and sometimes despite themselves. And
that's the way it went.

But under the surface, a lot of the common folk seethed and
simmered quietly. Especially the youth, who watched helplessly
as their few remaining rights and privileges slipped away, replaced
with ever more-demanding rules and restrictions.

I was a gangly, knock-kneed kid then, just entering my adoles-
cent years. And even though I wasn't directly involved, I heard the
murmurings of dissent, the stories swirling around me: The preachers did this, and they said that. How awful and unfair was that?

Did you hear? Now Elmo wants to outlaw volleyball. He

doesn't think boys and girls should play together because it might lead them to have lustful thoughts. Or some similar lunacy. It never stopped. And before I even had a chance to form my own opinions, any natural respect for the preachers and their edicts that I might have had was duly crushed.

My relationship with Dad wasn't much better.

My brothers and I hung together, in silent revolt against his rather strident admonitions. That's pretty much how he communicated with us. Not by discussion but by dictates.

And so he lost us, one by one, as we entered our teenage years.

Always frantically busy, always overwhelmed with his writing duties at Pathway, I don't know if he even noticed.

Of course, every once in a while one of us would do something wrong, and he would catch wind of it. Then he would launch into one of his long, angry lectures, and we would simply hunker down and take it, knowing that the storm would eventually pass.

And it always did. Within hours, he would be back at Pathway, absorbed in the details of his daily work. And we would return to our state of quiet rebellion. In retrospect, it was doomed to fail—his relationship with his sons. There was no way he could win.

Not after we were old enough.

Not after we could stand up to him.

Not after we could leave.

9

After Maggie and Jesse left, it was a great relief to my father when, at age nineteen, my brother Stephen decided to join the Amish church.

It's a huge deal, the decision to become a member and begin "following church," because among other things, it means that the chances of that person leaving are greatly diminished. All Amish parents pray that their children will make that choice. Unfortunately many Amish youth make the choice not of their own volition but to fulfill the expectations of those around them.

Joining the church takes about four months. On a Sunday morning, after the singing starts, the preachers get up and walk solemnly to a separate conference room, or Obrote. After the preachers leave the room, those who are taking instructions for baptism rise and follow them to the conference. There, the preachers admonish and instruct the applicants. After half an hour or so, the applicants return to the congregation. The preachers confer among themselves for another fifteen minutes or so, then rejoin the congregation.

During the time it takes to join, applicants must not only be on their best behavior but also be prepared to walk the gauntlet and take gratuitous swipes from anyone and everyone. To smile and accept even the most shallow yet stinging criticisms. Attitude is everything, and even the slightest sign of resentment might be enough to delay or even deny baptism and membership. Everyone scrutinizes the applicants closely, looking for the tiniest faults, and when admonished, the applicants must submit humbly. Promise to do better. And then walk the line even more flawlessly.

The pressure can become unbearable—especially if applicants are known for having engaged in rowdy behavior in the past. Then they are watched all the more closely—and admonished all the more incessantly.

Poor Stephen chafed under these conditions. He was constantly being rebuked: His hairstyle and sideburns were too worldly. His beard was too thin, too trimmed. And so forth, on and on.

Slowly, silently, he simmered. Until he could not take it anymore. At some point, in total secrecy, he began to plan his escape.

It all came down one fine winter day. My parents had left that morning with an English neighbor to do some shopping. They would be gone all day. My sisters, too, were gone. So only three brothers—Stephen, Titus, and I—were at home. We worked through the morning hours, and at noon, after eating, Stephen disappeared upstairs. There he packed a bag—some clothes, his meager stash of cash.

Then he left. Walking across the snow-covered fields to the south, through the woods to Highway 3. From there, he hitchhiked east. And just like that, he was gone.

Before he left, he handed Titus a note to give to Dad. That afternoon, Titus and I worked uneasily around the farm. We did our evening chores until darkness fell. Around six thirty or so, the car pulled in. Our parents had returned.

We helped carry in the day's haul: bags of groceries, store-bought ice cream for supper, even some candy and hardware items. Dad proudly unveiled a brand-new Homelite chain saw.

"So Stephen can cut wood with it," he said. Quickly busying ourselves with the bags and boxes that needed to be put away, neither Titus nor I responded.

The table was set for supper, and Mom bustled about, stirring a pot of soup on the stove. Then Titus nervously disappeared upstairs. When he returned, I knew he had the note. He approached Dad in the living room.

"Here's a note from Stephen," he said.

I felt very sorry for Titus, for the hard thing he had to do. It wasn't right that Stephen asked such a thing of his brother. But then again, what are brothers for, if not to do the occasional hard thing for you? Titus stood there bravely, unflinching, looking right at Dad.

"What . . . what do you mean?" Dad stuttered uncomprehendingly.

"A note," Titus repeated, thrusting it at Dad. "A note from Stephen. He left today."

"Ah, my. Oh, no," Dad groaned, his face darkening. Mom, sensing something was amiss, walked into the living room.

"What's wrong?" she asked sharply, sensing doom.

"Stephen left today," Dad told her. "We don't know where he is, or where he went."

I lurked behind a curtain in the living room and heard the exclamations of dismay and grief as my parents absorbed the news. Dad's face was twisted into a furious frown. Mom stood frozen in shock, mouth agape.

All the joy was gone—the treats they had brought us from

town, the ice cream and candy, the new chain saw. Dad proclaimed he wasn't hungry and stomped off to his office. Supper forgotten, her soup simmering forlornly on the stove, Mom walked about with heaving shoulders, sobbing and entreating no one in particular to tell her where her son had gone.

But no one could tell her. Because we didn't know.

Soon the news flashed through the community. Another of David Wagler's evil boys had left. Now he had lost three of his children to the world. First Maggie, then Jesse, and now Stephen. Everyone clucked. Why, Stephen had been taking instructions for baptism, with such vile plans lurking in his heart. How fortunate that he had not been baptized.

For my parents, it was one more embarrassing burden to bear. As it always is for Amish parents when a young son leaves. (Or a daughter, although daughters leave much less frequently.) Somehow, even though mostly unspoken, the feeling is that it reflects badly on the parents' abilities. And their methods of raising children. Maybe if they had been stricter, it wouldn't have happened. Maybe if they had broken their son's will way back when he was a child. Maybe this. Maybe that. The regrets, the mental guessing games never stop. When Stephen left, people in the Aylmer church offered sympathy, but who knows what they really thought? Or said among themselves.

Stephen ended up settling in Welland, a small town about an hour east of Aylmer, where he found a job in a factory. He came home to visit now and then, but only when he knew my parents wouldn't be around, and he vowed never to return home to stay—as long as we lived in Aylmer.

Dad, meanwhile, was in a real bind. Stephen was gone. Titus would be next—he was certain of it. And even though I was only fourteen, he knew that eventually my turn would come. So he made a decision: We would *all* leave.

Dad loved Aylmer. Of all the places he had ever lived, Aylmer was closest to his heart. Somehow, he connected with the place as he had connected with no other. Leaving was a hard and bitter pill for him, but eventually he gave in to the inevitable and did what he thought he needed to do to preserve his family. He decided to find another suitable community and move there.

And so, he and Mom took off on the Greyhound bus to find another place to live. They had heard of a fledgling settlement in south central Iowa called Bloomfield, so they went there. Checked out the available farms—and the church rules, of course. Shortly after they returned home, they went to visit again—this time accompanied by my brother Joseph and his wife. And this time, my father bought a three-hundred-acre farm in Bloomfield, two miles directly north of the small village of West Grove. Just across the old rickety wooden bridge that spanned the Fox River.

The news sent shock waves throughout the Amish world. The great man, the famous writer David Wagler, was leaving Aylmer. It was practically unfathomable, that's how closely his name was intertwined with Aylmer. Tongues wagged. People clucked. *He had wild sons. Couldn't control them.*

Now he was leaving the place he loved. Moving to the obscure, upstart settlement of Bloomfield, Iowa.

All to try to keep his remaining sons Amish.

We'll see how it goes.

We'll see if it works.

That's what they said.

And as if to mock their words and hidden thoughts, Stephen returned home and quietly got to work, getting ready for the move to Bloomfield. They knew, all those Aylmer people, that he planned to join the Amish church there. Officially, of course, they were happy for him. But silently, they seethed.

In September, Dad ended his time at *Family Life.* In the future, he would contribute as a writer, but he would no longer be editor. That job went to the young preacher Elmo Stoll, the de facto leader in Aylmer.

In his last editorial, my father said good-bye to his readers. Of course, in true Amish fashion, he carefully hinted at the *real* issues without actually addressing them. He said that he had devoted much of his time in the past to *Family Life*—to the point, he added, that he may have neglected a few other important things. Now it was time for him to devote himself to another kind of family life.

A nice play on words, his official statement. Fraught with symbolism, but pretty much devoid of meaning, at least to us—his family.

The Aylmer leaders and Dad's peers at Pathway supported his decision—at least publicly. They spoke kind words. "Come back and visit," they said. "And we'll come see you in Bloomfield, too." But privately, they all must have wondered why David Wagler could not control his wild, unruly sons.

● ● ●

I was fourteen, going on fifteen, that summer. It was an exciting time. And a little scary. I knew great changes were coming. I was about to leave the only home I had ever known. The only community. The only world. Not to mention all my friends.

Despite my excitement and anticipation, there was a strong sense of sadness, too. I knew that all too soon, in mere months, our lives would change forever.

But the date had been set, and there was no turning back. We planned to leave in late October 1976. My father had lived in Aylmer for twenty-three years, the longest he had lived uninterrupted at any place in his life. But he did not shrink from what must have been a gallingly difficult task. Instead, he solemnly and steadfastly wrapped up his business affairs and prepared to leave.

For my mother, too, leaving was a bittersweet thing. One doesn't live for twenty-three years in the same house, only to leave it blithely. She had seen and endured so much here. The place held a lifetime of memories for her. She had arrived with a family of five small children. Now there were eleven. Not all at home anymore, of course. But here, in this house, she had borne six children, mothered them, and befriended them.

Dad sold the farm that summer, and in early October, we held a sale. Dad's auctioneer friend, Les Shackleton, officiated—his trip-hammer voice booming from the portable speakers. A vast array of belongings had to be sold. Machinery, cattle, horses, buggies, household goods, general junk. It was a huge event. People came from miles away, from many surrounding communities, to attend the great disposal sale of David and Ida Mae Wagler's property. Even my brother Jesse quietly slipped home and hung around that day.

Later that month, two heavily loaded tractor trailers lumbered down the dusty gravel road and turned south toward Highway 3, leaving behind the only home I had ever known.

My childhood days—my Aylmer days—were over.

My youth and running-around days would be in Bloomfield, Iowa.

PART 2

10

As a child, I had always dreamed of driving a truck, a big old 18-wheeler, and hauling loads for days and weeks at a time along endless highways through distant lands. The trip from Aylmer to Bloomfield on that tractor trailer was, alas, as close as I ever got to realizing my truck-driver dream. Perched in the sleeper, I watched through the windshield, determined not to miss a thing. On and on we drove into the night, and then into the dawn.

After an exhilarating twenty-six-hour journey, during which I slept all of about two minutes, we finally approached Bloomfield, and the two tractor trailers slowly lumbered down the long drive of our new farm.

Our new home sat nestled on the south side of rolling hills, bordered by acres of woods to the west, pasture fields dotted with huge old oaks to the north, and the Fox River to the south.

The house was a tiny ranch. A large, sagging, ramshackle barn stood a few hundred yards away, and several ragged outbuildings lay scattered here and there. The centerpiece of the property was a brand-new dairy barn that had been raised a few months before by an all-Amish crew, complete with a brand-new stave silo that had been shipped in from Madison, Wisconsin.

Within a few hours, all our belongings were unloaded. The men carried the heavy furniture, mattresses, and boxes inside, while my mom and sisters directed everything to its proper spot.

It seemed surreal. After weeks and months of planning and high anticipation, here we were at a new home, in a strange new world. Aylmer was now forever behind us. The life I had known from birth was gone. Whatever the future held, it would flow from this place. It was impossible, at that moment, to absorb the enormity of that realization.

•　•　•

Bloomfield was a young community back then, consisting of only twenty or so families. It had been founded just a few short years before, in the early 1970s, by Gideon Yutzy and his sons. In terms of rules and restrictions, Bloomfield was moderate, kind of like Aylmer. One rule I didn't like was the mandate of "steel-rimmed wheels only" for buggies. In Aylmer, we had rubber-covered rims on the buggy wheels. I know that seems like a small thing, but it really makes a huge difference, both in wear and tear on the buggy and in terms of noise. Steel-rimmed wheels rattle and creak a lot more, and the horse has to work harder to pull the load.

But I digress.

Gradually, other families had trickled in from settlements in various states, and before long, Bloomfield became a fashionable destination for outcasts, misfits, and malcontents from other, mostly larger, communities. Families had come from fairly progressive places like Kokomo, Indiana, and Arthur, Illinois, and from such regressive areas as Fortuna, Missouri, and Buchanan County, Iowa. And from every shade between.

It was fall when we came. Late October. The mornings were white with frost, and the farmers were harvesting their crops. And over the course of those first few weeks, we quickly established a routine and rhythm of life in this new place.

Rhoda and Nathan trudged off each day to the little Amish schoolhouse, two miles away. Stephen, Titus, and I worked hard from dawn till dusk milking cows, plowing the fields, and repairing the tattered remnants of old rusty fences.

One of our first critical tasks was to enlarge the house. We staked out and built two wide new wings. A larger kitchen for Mom on one end. Bedrooms for the girls on the other. And a larger basement. Our days were so busy that we didn't really have much time to get homesick for our old world of Aylmer.

All in all, we really liked Bloomfield. Things seemed more relaxed here. Less tweaking of the rules than there had been in Aylmer. And even though there were vast cultural differences among those who had moved here, the leaders seemed to have a pretty good grip on things—at least early on.

We assimilated with our new peers pretty easily, though we quickly realized that the people of Bloomfield were not like those in Aylmer. These people had emerged from varied communities with strange customs and even stranger surnames. Names like Lambright, Beachy, Hochstedler, Gingerich, and Yutzy. To us they sounded funny. But these people were real. And they seemed cool enough. Mostly, anyway.

That made for an interesting mix of young people. I was a part of this group. These were my people. And although I sometimes felt detached and alone, I mingled, immersed myself in the vibrant details of life around me.

I enjoyed the singings, mostly. The buggies clattering as we gathered, around six thirty or so, on a Sunday night. Small knots of youth drifting toward the house, where supper would be served. Hanging with my buddies as we gathered. The house father calling everyone to attention and all heads bowing for silent prayer.

Then the serious business of eating the evening meal: mashed potatoes, noodles, some form of hamburger-laced casserole, baked beans, potato salad, and bread. Then dessert and coffee and more hanging out, with boisterous talk, local gossip (who was dating whom), and conversation about hunting, fishing and trapping, or work on the farm.

As eight o'clock approached, my friends and I often filed back into the house early, so as to grab the treasured back bench against the wall. There were two reasons for this: We'd have a wall to lean against, and we could get away with more monkeyshines. Bloomfield didn't use tables at the singings, just rows of benches. A row of boys, a row of girls, a row of boys, a row of girls.

At 8:00 sharp, the first song was announced. As the minutes crept by, we sang and sang. It seemed to me sometimes, as the harmony swelled and my spirit soared, that I could never leave, never forsake this ancient heritage, this priceless legacy. That no sacrifice would be too great to draw these things inside and keep them in my heart.

Shortly before nine thirty someone announced and led the parting song. After its last notes faded, the young men got up from the benches and walked out single file. The singing was over for one more week.

We milled about outside. Socialized and chatted for a while. Those who were dating were the first to hurry away. In Bloomfield, courting couples tended to leave posthaste for the girl's house, because dates were decreed over at midnight.

Then, one by one, my friends and I hitched up our horses and left, a long convoy of buggies with blinking orange lights.

• • •

Gradually, even more families arrived. Bloomfield was suddenly the "hot" place to be. And soon enough, the single district was bulging at the seams.

It had gotten too big.

And that meant only one thing: It was time to divide it.

Every Amish district must have its own contingent of at least two preachers and a deacon. A newly created district meant there would have to be ordinations to fill these positions.

And so it was decided. A dividing line separating the two districts was drawn, and an ordination was scheduled. As the day drew nearer, the young married men in the community grew increasingly somber and burdened.

Church was at our house the Sunday of the ordination. The winds whipped and swirled that afternoon, and storm clouds gathered. Inside, a large group of people were sitting in row upon row of wooden benches. We were having a Communion service, or "Big Church," as we called it. It was an all-day affair.

But this particular service was different, because at the end, a new preacher would be ordained. Every corner of the house pulsed with palpable tension.

Near the close of the service, Bishop George, a slight, bald man with a long gray beard, stood to recite the rules of ordination. He explained that he and the other preachers would retire to a separate side room (which happened to be my parents' bedroom). Then one preacher would open the door a crack and place his ear in the opening. Members would vote by whispering their choices into the preacher's ear, and a tally would be taken. Any married man with three or more votes would be in the lot.

With that, Bishop George and the preachers retreated to my

parents' room and closed the door, and the voting began. The older men went first. Walked up to the door, paused briefly, then whispered their choices before returning to their seats. After that, according to age, younger married men, then young unmarried men, married women, and finally, single women.

Not being a member, I didn't vote. My buddies and I took a break from our normal wisecracking and watched somberly. No surly antics. No smart-aleck actions. No smirks. The air was heavy, oppressive.

The voting took awhile. Then, after the last member had voted, the door shut on the cloistered preachers while they tallied the votes. Minutes passed. Then Deacon Menno popped out of the side-room door, gathered five songbooks, and popped back in. Everyone pretended not to notice, but all eyes took a careful count: five songbooks. There would be five men in the lot.

Minutes later, the preachers filed out in somber procession and took their seats on the bench along the wall. The tension escalated. Deacon Menno arranged the songbooks on a little table. Each book was tied shut with a thin white string.

Then Bishop George stood and cleared his throat. "There are five brothers in the lot," he announced in his high, squeaky voice. "They are . . ." and he slowly, concisely pronounced the five names. Each man sagged visibly as he heard his name.

Then slowly, one by one, they got up and walked the long path to the table. Each man chose a book and then took a seat on the bench before the table. Five books. Five men. Everyone waiting.

After a short prayer, Bishop George slowly approached the bench where the five men sat. He took the book from the first, untied the white string, and opened it.

Nothing.

The first man almost collapsed with relief.

Bishop George then took the book from the next man's trembling hands. Fumbled with the string. Opened the book.

Again, nothing.

The three remaining men viewed the situation with increasing alarm and accelerating heartbeats. No one moved. No one breathed. Original odds were one to five. Now they were one to three. Bishop George approached the third man and held out his hand. Took the book. Untied the string. Opened it.

Again, nothing.

Now it was down to one of the remaining two. Two young men. What passed through their minds at that instant remains known only to them and God. They sat there, frozen. Mercifully, Bishop George did not prolong their agony. He approached the fourth man and held out his hand. Took the book. Untied the string. Opened it.

Inside the book, on page 770, was a little slip of white paper. Bishop George's hand shook slightly as he took the little slip of paper. He looked down at the young man before him and pointed his right index finger, signifying, You are the one.

The young man struggled to his feet. And there, before us all, Bishop George ordained him, proclaiming him a minister of the gospel from that day forth until his death.

The young man briefly lost control of his emotions; his body shook with quick, choppy sobs. But just as quickly, he recovered and stood there quietly, his head bowed, as he accepted the office and the duties he would henceforth carry.

The other men in the lot, vastly relieved at the outcome, now clustered around the young man who had just been ordained and comforted him. The preachers, too, all of them, came and welcomed him into their midst.

Then it was over. The congregation was dismissed. The young

man sat down on the bench. He looked around him, at all the shadowy figures meshing in a hazy blur.

He was now a preacher.

Until his death.

His life would never be the same. *Never.*

Nor, for that matter, would my family's. The young man ordained that day was my oldest brother, Joseph.

And that's how it all comes down. An Amish man gets up in the morning, a regular member of the church, goes to the service with his wife and children, and returns home that evening, ordained to the ministry for the rest of his life.

A preacher.

Lots of work for no pay.

Just like that.

The process is based on the New Testament account of the choosing of Matthias by lot to replace Judas after he betrayed Jesus. The whole thing takes less than an hour. There is no counseling session, no discussion with the ordained to see whether or not he even *has* a calling. It's the only system the Amish have ever used.

It has its flaws, but overall, it works amazingly well. A quiet young man who has never had much to say is ordained, and one month later, with no training whatsoever, gets up to preach for the first time. It's sink or swim, and somehow, he swims. And over the course of many years, he develops into a gifted speaker and a powerful preacher.

Of course, sometimes the reverse is also true. I've heard many a sermon from preachers who could not speak publicly to save their lives. Men who spent the first ten minutes of their sermons bemoaning the "heavy burden" of their calling. Men who, in my opinion, should never have been ordained. But the lot chose them, just as it chose Matthias. Granted, nothing more is ever written of Matthias, other than the fact that he was ordained by lot. So perhaps he wasn't that great a speaker either.

My brother Joseph, it turned out, was a swimmer. He soon developed into the premier preacher in Bloomfield. When he stood to preach, the congregation sat alert, absorbed in his message, and much to the children's delight, he always stopped on time.

For me, the other preachers suddenly seemed more human, because now my brother was one of them. And to Joseph's credit, although he strongly disapproved of my subsequent life choices, he was always there for me through the turmoil that would characterize the next ten years.

11

It's a law of human nature. The young will defy and test the previous generation's boundaries and push them to the limits. It has always been so and will likely always be.

This is particularly true in the Amish culture, with its austere lifestyle, where the rules prohibit all things modern and, therefore, sinful: cars, radios, and television.

Very few young Amish kids with a spark of life and an ounce of willpower will simply accept their leaders' admonitions not to touch "unclean things." Most need to experiment, experience, and decide for themselves.

My friends and I were no different.

There were six of us.

Marvin and Rudy Yutzy were my first and closest friends in Bloomfield. They were first cousins and had known each other all their lives. I was the new guy on their turf, but they gladly made room for me.

Rudy, the youngest—and yet somehow the tallest—was the orator of the group. He could weave and stitch and thread the most fascinating, vivid tales from the most mundane, everyday events. No detail was too small. No comment too obscure. He included and expounded on everything in fantastic, colorful narratives that flowed in a continual rolling stream.

Marvin was a bit more reserved. He was intelligent, thoughtful, and observant, with a keen, dry sense of humor. He could deadpan a joke and move on before the true incisive humor of his observation ever hit you.

Then there were the Herschberger brothers—Willis and Vern—who moved to Bloomfield from the large, troubled settlement of Arthur, Illinois, about a year after we arrived. They were tough, cynical, talkative, friendly, and extremely knowledgeable in the ways of the world.

Mervin Gingerich's family had been one of the first to move to Bloomfield. Mervin was my age—a muscular hunk of a kid with a ready smile and a round, perpetually red face. His father was Bishop George Gingerich, so his family had excellent standing in the community.

Me? Well, I'm not quite sure where I fit in. I was the one who brooded and mulled things over. Or perhaps overmulled is more accurate, if that's a word. I was the one who spoke the occasional comment that made absolutely no sense to the others. Tall, skinny, a beanpole of a kid with a ready smile, I was intensely loyal to my friends.

The six of us met in Bloomfield, and somehow we were drawn to one another. We were intelligent and hungry for knowledge. We read voraciously, mostly trashy bestsellers—picked up at yard sales and used-book stores—that we kept carefully stashed under our mattresses or in little nooks about the house.

We were an exclusive group, a tight nucleus, huddled together and protecting one another from the storms that occasionally engulfed us.

Looking back, I can't remember any time in my life when I felt closer to a group of friends than I did to those five guys.

Things were pretty calm at first. We were, for the most part, decent kids. Bloomfield had no wild youth.

Sad to say, this placid state would not survive for long. It couldn't. Because we harbored in our hearts the seeds of rebellion. Or maybe it was the seeds of life, of adventure, of freedom. Perhaps it was a little of both.

We wanted to experience the things we saw around us, things outside our sheltered world. Things we'd read about and heard of, things we'd seen others do, things that happened in other communities.

We were young and full of spirit.

We were sixteen.

● ● ●

Sixteen.

The gateway to manhood in Amish culture.

And sixteen is a hard, bright line. One day you're fifteen and a child. The next morning you're sixteen and a man. Well, maybe not a man, but something more than a child, something more than you were the day before.

And the six of us? Well, we were simply spirited youth. That doesn't excuse a lot of the stuff we pulled off, but who can instruct a pack of youth who band together in revolt? At that age? No one.

And no one did.

We knew instinctively that there was so much more beyond our closed and structured world, so much just waiting for us to grasp and feel and taste and absorb.

But it wasn't only that the outside world drew us. We were also repelled by what we saw and heard around us every day. Most of the adults—those securely anchored in the faith—didn't seem any too happy in their daily lives. In fact, they were mostly downright grumpy. There was little in our own world that attracted us, made us stop and think, *That's what I want. To live like that.*

We were stuck in a stifling, hostile culture consisting of myriad complex rules and restrictions. More things were forbidden than were allowed. And that's not to mention the drama, the dictatorial decrees, the strife among so-called brothers, and the seemingly endless emotional turmoil that resulted. We had seen and lived it all.

And even though it would have been difficult, if not impossible, for us to articulate, there burned inside each of us a spark of deep desire and longing *not* to be different from the outside world. From English society. *Not* to wear galluses and those awful homemade, barn-door pants. *Not* to have haircuts that looked as if someone had snipped around the edges of a bowl upended on our heads.

We longed to drive a car or truck, not a horse and buggy. We hungered for freedom, real freedom, unrestricted by a host of arcane laws based on tradition.

And we knew that when our fathers were young, they had done the very things they were now denying us. Not that they ever admitted any such thing. But we knew. And they should have known that we knew.

Don't do as I did is what we heard. *Do as I say.*

There was no tolerance for anything less than that, no attempt to consider our perspectives. No respect, no communication, no honesty. And that simply could not work in the age-old conflict between fathers and sons. Not when the sons have a shred of spirit.

And so, it was with that state of mind that I officially entered my Rumspringa years.

12

RUMSPRINGA. That mispronounced word popularized by the 2002 documentary film *Devil's Playground*, which, to be fair, was a pretty accurate depiction in many ways. The term *Rumspringa* simply means "running around."

All Amish youth run around. That's what they do after turning sixteen, when they are considered adults. Run with the youth and attend singings and social gatherings.

But if someone asked me what percentage of Amish youth "run wild" and touch and taste the unclean things of the outside world, either while they are at home or after leaving, my guess would be 20 to 25 percent. But that's just a guess. It might be close; it might not. Rumspringa varies greatly from community to community. Some smaller communities have almost no wild youth. In larger communities, wild youth are much more common.

Despite the fact that the producers of the documentary had unprecedented access to northern Indiana's wild Amish youth,

Devil's Playground left viewers with a huge misconception: the belief that the Amish actually allow their youth a time to explore, to run wild, to live a mainstream lifestyle. To decide whether or not they really want to remain Amish.

I'm not saying that never happens. It probably does, in some rare individual families. But church policy never approves it. It never has been that way and never will be. In fact, the Amish church does everything in its power to maintain its grip on the youth, including applying some of the most guilt-based pressure tactics in existence anywhere in the world. After all, there's no sense encouraging young people to taste the outside world, because there's a good chance they might not return—regardless of how good their intentions might have been when they left.

The smaller communities keep a tight grip on their youth. Or try to. That's why they're smaller communities, because the people there usually fled the larger settlements to get away from the wild-youth practices.

In Aylmer, if you looked sideways the wrong way, the leaders would whack you hard. Shave your beard? The deacon would be knocking on your door. Smoking, drinking, partying, or carousing? Absolutely unheard of in all its history.

Bloomfield used to have a similar iron grip on things, until six young men shattered the old molds and forged their own way.

And things have never been quite the same since.

• • •

We didn't consider ourselves "wild." In fact, we scorned anyone who consciously tried to be. And we didn't necessarily think we were cool. But we were, at least in our own restricted little world.

We simply did the ordinary, acceptable things that all Amish kids do.

Avid hunters, we tramped through cornfields and pastures in pursuit of pheasant and quail. And in season, we hunted deer from before dawn until dusk. Our successes were rare but greatly savored. The stories of our great feats were told and retold, and grew more fantastic with each telling.

At night, full of the vigor and energy of youth, we crashed through fields and the thick underbrush on wooded lots, following the baying of our coonhounds. Waiting for the excited chop of the hounds after a coon was treed. Rushing up with our flashlights and rifles, the crack of the .22, and the plop of the body as the coon fell from the tree to be attacked by the ravenous hounds. Somehow it was fun. For us, those were good, clean activities, and we enjoyed them to the fullest.

But acceptable activities like hunting and staying out late, while fun, simply weren't enough, maybe precisely because they were acceptable. And so the battle lines were drawn: the six of us against the world. Or at least against our world.

We were restless, driven by the pride and passions of youth, and unsure of what we really wanted, and we set out on a path of our own choosing. We weren't particularly rough or rowdy, but we did like to party a bit and have a good time.

On Sunday afternoons, we hung out at the park, sipping beer that we'd bought from Bea, the clerk at the little convenience store in Drakesville. And we smoked cigarettes, not necessarily because we enjoyed it, but just because we thought it looked cool to smoke.

Among each other, hanging out, we told rowdy jokes. Mimicked the preachers with mock sermons while laughing uncontrollably. And, of course, dismembered our adversaries with bold talk. And that's what it was, mostly. Brash, noisy, bold talk. Sometimes we even showed up a bit tipsy at the singings. Made all kinds of unfortunate scenes with our loud hilarity, much to the horror of the house father and other stodgy guests.

Sometimes, when there was no opposing traffic on the road, we raced our buggies. The challenger would pull up close behind, then lurch out to pass, gradually releasing the reins until the horses opened up into full stride, side by side, at breakneck speed, the buggies rocking dangerously, the horses straining with every possible ounce of muscle and sweat, until one buggy or the other pulled ahead and the loser conceded.

And, of course, we all harbored contraband—transistor radios and eight-track tape players. Getting caught with such contraband had definite and potentially severe consequences. At the very least, whatever was found would be confiscated, and the owner would receive a good stiff bawling out.

One weeknight, after running around with my buddies, I got home very late, probably around two or three in the morning. I was tired, and I made the mistake of leaving my tape player in the buggy, along with our collection of tapes, which we kept stashed in a fifty-pound paper Nutrena Feeds bag.

The next morning after breakfast, when I reached into the back of the buggy to retrieve the feed bag, it was gone. Dad must have been on the prowl bright and early. I figured he must have seized the bag and burned it in our water heater stove.

He never said a word to me, just smiled a secret little smile. There were probably thirty or forty tapes in the bag, two or three hundred dollars' worth—an accumulation of much furtive buying and trading, now reduced to ashes.

I was highly irritated—furious, actually—but did not even bother to confront my father. Instead, the following week, I seized one of Dad's old shotguns, a Savage pump-action 12-gauge with a tendency to misfire. I took it to Jim's Auction House in town, sold it for $150. Kept the money. And smiled a secret smile. I figured Dad and I were about even.

As our little group of six developed a rather tough, unsavory reputation throughout the Bloomfield settlement, we got bolder. We stepped over the lines, daring the preachers to come after us. Of course, we were careful never to step too far. We just kept nudging those lines, always applying pressure just over the acceptable boundaries.

Every once in a while, the older youth tried to straighten us up. Lectured us and admonished us not to act so silly.

"Stop trying to be so wild."

Their efforts were entirely fruitless. And it got so that most people just left us alone—except for our parents and the preachers. They never stopped lecturing, and they never stopped scolding. The problem was, they never told us why we needed to behave.

Everything was preached from a solid foundation of what had always been. Amish this. Amish that. We live this way because that's the way it is. We live this way because it's the way our fathers lived. We live this way, and we walk this path because it's the only way, the only path we've ever known.

It was our birthright. We were special—the chosen ones who preserved and honored "the only true way."

With some prodding, there might be a reluctant admission that yes, others not of our particular faith *might* make it to heaven, but only because they were not born Amish and didn't know any better. Those who *were* born in the faith had better stay, or they would surely face a terrible Judgment Day. That's what we heard. What we were told by our parents and what we heard in the sermons at church.

But they never explained why. Why we were special. Why we alone knew the only true path. Only that we were and we did.

That sure made for some messed-up minds and messed-up lives. Not for the drones—those who accepted without question what they were told. But for anyone with a speck of spirit, it could get a little crazy.

Think about it. You are in a box—a comfortable box, but a pretty confining one. You wonder what's outside. You peek out a bit now and then, and peer around. But deep down, you know that if you step outside that box, you are speeding directly down the highway to hell and could arrive at any instant. Boom, just like that.

That kind of pressure is a brutal thing, really, a severe mental strain. And it's the reason that in most communities, when Amish kids run wild, they usually run hard and mean. Because once that line is crossed, there are no others. Nothing they can do, short of returning, can make any difference.

Believe otherwise, as do the Mennonites and the Beachy Amish, who drive cars and prattle on about being saved, and the devil's got you right where he wants you.

That's what we were taught and what we believed.

• • •

Compared to what goes on in many other communities, my friends and I were pretty harmless, really. We weren't destructive. We didn't terrorize people. But somehow, we managed to frequently trigger a great outpouring of dramatic groans and intonations from parent and preacher alike: "How could my son act so wickedly?"

"Dee boova sind so loppich. So veesht." (The boys are so naughty. So wicked.)

"You know better. Why can't you just be good and behave like other boys? Such decent boys, so nice, and such upstanding members of the church."

They were nice and upstanding, all right. And utterly dull.

We gagged at such drama. Ignored the incessant scolding. Despised the pious boys. Hunkered down and persisted in our "wicked" ways. The more our parents and the preachers tried to crack down and suppress us, the harder we "kicked against the goads." Whatever discipline they designed and threw at us, we resisted. They plugged a leak here; the water slipped through over there. They tried to separate and divide, and it drew us that much closer to one another.

I'm not condoning—or bemoaning—what we did. It's just the way it was. And history is not undone just because one pretends it didn't happen or destroys the evidence.

And yet somehow when I look back on those times, I can't bring myself to be too harsh on anyone involved on either side. Oh sure, on occasion I can still dredge up mild resentment at a few pious, nosy, long-bearded busybodies who made a mission of trying to straighten out other people's kids. Who secretly harbored their own dark skeletons in their own closets. But overall, the years have tempered the rage and frustrations of our youth. And, I hope, softened the deep pain we inflicted on those closest to us at the time.

Although far from perfect, our parents had given up a lot. They had uprooted their lives. Moved to this new settlement in hopes of establishing a community where the youth would be respectful and behave, not drag in all the bad stuff, the wicked habits practiced in other places. I couldn't see that then. I can now.

And looking back, not that far from the age my father was at the time, I remember the vast chasm that separated us. The harsh, hollow words that echoed in anger and sadness across the great divide. Words spoken but not heard. Words better left unsaid. I was a hothead, strong willed and filled with passion, rage, and desire. Stubborn. Driven. As was he. I was my father's son.

I misbehaved. He fumed and hollered.

I seethed. He lectured and fussed.

I sulked. He watched and worried.

Mostly though, our communication was pretty much non-existent.

In reality, my father had reason to be concerned. He knew all too well the blood that ran through me—blood that could never be tamed by force, only by choice—and a will that would not bend.

He knew. He wouldn't have admitted it, or ever told me. But he knew.

Perhaps he felt a slight chill inside, a silent premonition of what was to come. Or maybe he actually believed it would all work out now that we had moved away from Aylmer—that the sacrifices he'd made would be rewarded.

If he did—he was wrong.

Tensions flared and faded between us, as confrontation after confrontation surged and subsided. The mental strain escalated to an almost unbearable level.

13

GARY SIMMONS, A SQUAT, CHUNKY YOUNG MAN dressed in western clothes, a wide-brimmed cowboy hat, and boots with spurs, showed up unannounced at our farm one day with Trader Don, the local horse dealer. Don introduced him to us as Gary Simmons, a rancher, in the area looking to buy some horses.

Gary shook hands with a firm grip and looked you in the eye. He spoke with a distinct western accent and had a great booming laugh. His pretty, young wife, Joyce, stuck close to his side and smiled.

Dad didn't really have any suitable horses to sell, that much was decided in about two minutes. Our horses were a pretty raggedy bunch. Don and Gary hung around and chatted. Eventually Dad drifted away, back to the office and his typewriter, where he was pounding out his next article for *Family Life*. Soon, I was the only one standing there talking to Don and Gary. Turns out Gary hailed from Valentine, Nebraska, and managed a ranch there.

I asked him about it. How big was the ranch?

Fifteen thousand acres, he said. He ran the ranch for a group of cattle investors from Kansas.

Wow. Fifteen thousand acres. The number boggled my mind.

Then, quietly, out of Trader Don's hearing, I asked, "Do you ever have any use for some good help out there?" I don't know why I asked, but I did. I didn't really have any plans or anything.

Gary chuckled. "Oh, you bet," he answered. "If you ever need a job, call me. We always have an opening for good help. We can always use another good hand."

Soon after that, they left. I mulled over what he had said about needing good help. Maybe, just maybe, one day I would call him.

It's not that I particularly liked horses or considered myself a horseman. But like most teenagers, I had often dreamed of being a real cowboy. I'd seen the pictures, read the Westerns—stories by Louis L'Amour. Zane Grey. Max Brand. Before, it had always been a minor dream, but now a doorway had cracked open. It might not be a bad experience, to head out west and work on a ranch.

The idea, and the beginnings of a plan, had been planted.

One evening about six months later, from the phone at the local Amish schoolhouse, I called Gary Simmons at his ranch.

• • •

Somehow I slept, though fitfully, waking now and again to glance at the tiny alarm clock beside my bed. The entire house slumbered in silence.

I dozed off for a time and then jolted awake again. The little fluorescent hands on the alarm clock glowed eerily. Two o'clock. One last time, I slid my hand beneath my pillow and felt for the note. It was still there, exactly where I'd placed it last night after scribbling it on a scrap of paper the day before and where my father would find it at dawn.

Quietly, slowly, so as not to wake my brothers, I shifted in the bed, lifted the covers, and stepped onto the cool concrete floor. I felt my way through the pitch-black darkness to the door, opened it, and slipped out of the bedroom.

I took a few quick, quiet steps to the left, into the furnace room, which housed my father's great brick-and-steel contraption of a homemade wood-burning stove. Dug around in the large lidded wooden box where Mom stored her winter blankets. Located the little black duffel bag I'd packed the day before, lifted it out, and set it on the floor.

Then I slipped into the clothes I had hidden away—a plain, old green shirt and a newer pair of denim barn-door pants. No galluses. Where I was going, I wouldn't need them. I laced my feet into a pair of tough leather work boots and then picked up the duffel bag. I was ready.

Upstairs, on the main floor of the house, my parents slept, unaware. With a keen ear for any unusual sounds, I walked softly to the door, gently turned the knob, and pulled it open, oh so slowly. The hinges protested in a faint, almost imperceptible squeak. I stepped outside into the night and quietly pulled the door shut behind me.

Once I was outside, Jock, our faithful mutt, met me. He seemed surprised and a little startled, but he made no sound.

"Shhh, Jock. Good boy," I whispered. He shook himself and wagged his tail, whimpering excitedly. Leaning down, I scratched his ears in farewell.

Into the darkness I went, down the concrete walks and out the drive. There was no moon that night and no stars. I had no flashlight, so I could barely see, but my eyes gradually adjusted as I continued on my way, out the long half-mile lane to the road, the gravel crunching beneath my feet.

Halfway out, I passed my oldest brother, Joseph's, house. It loomed dark and quiet. And then it, too, was behind me.

Finally I reached the gravel road. I paused for the first time and turned. Took one last look across the fields to the house where my family slept. The kerosene lamp Mom kept burning at night flickered dimly through the kitchen windows.

Then I turned my face to the south and walked. There should be no traffic on a deserted country road at this early morning hour. At least that's what I hoped. Two miles. That's how far it was. Two miles to the highway and to freedom.

I walked into the night, my senses honed to their finest edge. In my eager mind, the great shining vistas of distant horizons gleamed and beckoned. A world that would fulfill the deep yearning, the nebulous shifting dreams of a hungry, driven youth. And it would be mine, all of it, to pluck from the forbidden tree and taste and eat. I could not know that night of the long, hard road that stretched into infinity before me. That I was lost. I could not know of the years of turmoil, rage, and anguish that eventually would push me to the brink of madness and despair.

And so I strode on through the night, crunching along the gravel road, the duffel bag swinging at my side. Up the steep hill, down, and then up again past the crossroads leading to the schoolhouse. Far ahead, the lights of West Grove flickered in the darkness. To the left stood an old graveyard filled with silent, looming tombstones. Focusing straight ahead, I continued to walk, past the old church on the left and Chuck's Café on the right. Then on to Highway 2.

Other than a few pole lights along the highway, it was pitch black. There was no traffic. None at all. I turned east and walked the final quarter mile to my buddy Dewayne's house.

Dewayne Cason had moved to West Grove from Ottumwa a few years before. In his upper twenties, Dewayne was a tobacco-chewing mule skinner whose favorite activity was hunting coon at night on muleback. I had tagged along with him from time to time, bumping along on the back of one of his trusty mules, following his baying hounds as they trailed and treed the occasional coon. Every once in a while he would give me odd jobs around his little farm, paying me a few bucks here and there to help him out. He was a colorful character and a good friend.

Dewayne worked at the John Deere factory in Ottumwa and drove twenty-some miles back and forth every day. When I first made plans to leave, I asked him if he could take me along one morning and drop me off at the bus station. He readily agreed, probably thinking nothing would ever come of it. But my plans jelled, and I told him I'd be there Tuesday morning.

He was the only person, other than myself, who knew of my plans. I didn't even tell my buddies. It was too dangerous. If it were discovered that they had known my plans and remained silent, they'd get in serious trouble. It was simply not safe to tell anyone. I had hinted about the thing I was considering, but I never told anyone in my Amish world of my actual plans. Not a soul.

I walked up to Dewayne's darkened house at about three thirty. So far, so good. I had met not a single car in the two-plus-mile walk. In the house, everyone was sleeping. I sat on the steps of Dewayne's front porch and waited, clutching my duffel bag. An hour passed. Then two. Light flickered in the eastern sky. Sunrise. About now, they would be waking up back home. About now, my note would have been found. A tinge of fear flashed through me. I was only two miles away. What if Dad decided to come up to West Grove and look for me? Come on, Dewayne.

I heard him then, bumping about inside. He opened the door, saw me, and then hollered back inside to his wife, Debbie, "He's here."

From inside, Debbie, who was due any day with their second child, said something I couldn't understand.

Dewayne had slept in and was running late, but we eventually got into his old beater pickup and roared east on the highway to Route 63, through Bloomfield, then north, toward Ottumwa. Dewayne mumbled and swore about how he would be late for work. "Of all mornings to have to drop someone at the bus station."

When we finally arrived in Ottumwa, he pulled up to the bus depot and braked. "Take it easy, Bud," he said, extending his hand. "And good luck." I grasped it, thanked him, and stepped out with my duffel bag. He roared away to his job at the John Deere factory.

Hope he doesn't get written up for being late, I thought.

I walked into the station and, half timid, half scared, approached the counter. "How much for a ticket to Sioux City, Iowa?" I asked. After handing the man behind the counter just shy of thirty bucks, I realized that the bus would be leaving in about an hour. So, with my ticket clutched firmly in my hand, I sat on a bench in the station and waited.

And waited.

I was totally focused on what lay ahead. Not once did the thought cross my mind that I should just give it up and go back home. Not once. My only fear was that Dad would hire a driver, rush up to Ottumwa, and intercept me. I wasn't sure I'd have the strength to face him down. He might compel me to return. So I waited, fearfully scanning the street now and then for any sign of him.

The hour passed, and then, finally, the bus pulled up outside and hissed to a halt. I walked up, stepped through the sliding door, and gave the driver my ticket. A few minutes later, the bus shuddered and slid out of the parking lot, onto the street, through town, and then to the highway.

I was out. Free. I wondered—fleetingly—what was going on

back home. But not much. I was too excited. I looked out the window at the rolling landscape as the bus rumbled along through town after town, stopping at stations here and there. Noon came and went, and by midafternoon, we approached Sioux City and pulled into the station. I got off and inquired about the next bus to Valentine, Nebraska. It would leave the next day, about midmorning. I bought a ticket and then walked around town to find a motel room.

I had left home with one hundred and fifty dollars, money from a horse I had recently sold. Well, it was a small horse, a half pony, really. And it was worth much more than that, but I needed the money to get away, so I took what I could get.

I found a ramshackle motel and booked a room, my first stay at any motel. It was a hovel, really—cheap, smelly, and damp. But to me, it seemed like a great, grand thing, a huge adventure—a motel room in a big city.

My lodging for the night secured, it was time to venture out and buy some clothes. My shirts were fine, I figured. But I really wanted to get rid of those barn-door pants. I walked around downtown, gawking through store windows until I spotted a clothing store. When I walked in, the worn hardwood floor creaked under my feet.

The clerk was a middle-aged man with a tiny gray mustache. He was stooped over a bit from years of service on the floor.

"I need a pair of jeans," I told him.

"Certainly," he replied, smiling. He showed me shelves loaded with stack after stack of blue jeans. But I had a problem. I had no idea what size I wore. Timidly, I mentioned that fact to him.

I'm sure it must have seemed strange to him that I didn't even know my own size, but he didn't blink an eye. Instead, he just smiled kindly, pawed through the piles of jeans, pulled out a few different sizes, and held them up to my waist.

"I'd suggest you try this size," he said. 32 x 32. I took the jeans from him and walked into a fitting room. Down went the barn-door pants. And for the first time in my life, I slipped into a pair of store-bought English jeans—Lee brand—with a real zipper in front.

They were probably a little short, but I didn't know any better. I thought they fit perfectly. *Real blue jeans.* I admired myself in the mirror. Then I walked out of the fitting room, picked up another pair the same size, bought them both, and walked proudly out the door and back to my motel. For the first time ever, I was not conscious that I was any different from anyone else around me, because I wasn't—except for my haircut. But I would get that taken care of soon enough. I felt great. This was definitely something I could get used to.

I spent the evening watching TV in my motel room—a huge treat. I finally drifted off to sleep, trusting that I'd wake up in due time the next morning. I knew nothing of wake-up calls from the front desk. That night I slumbered, exhausted from lack of sleep and the tension of the previous night. And somehow I blocked it all out—everything I'd left behind at home. I managed not to think about my parents—especially my mother, who was undoubtedly worried, sick to death, not knowing where I was.

I was seventeen years old. A minor. And I had pulled it off. I had just left home. Run away in the middle of the night.

14

THE NEXT MORNING I BOARDED A BUS and headed west into Nebraska. The rolling farmland flowed past outside, followed by the sand hills of the north central part of the state. By late afternoon, we pulled into Valentine. Clutching my duffel bag, I stepped off the bus and looked around hopefully. No one was waiting.

I had called Gary the week before and told him I was coming. Where was he? I waited nervously in the bus station for about fifteen minutes. Then a Suburban pulled in and parked. A short, burly man in a cowboy hat got out. He swaggered up to the door. It was Gary. I walked outside, and he grasped my hand.

"Welcome," he said, smiling. We walked to where Gary's wife and three young daughters sat waiting. "Are you hungry?" he asked. "How about the Pizza Hut?"

Of course I was hungry. A young Amish kid is always hungry, and Pizza Hut sounded just fine.

"I'd like that."

After eating, we headed out to the ranch, thirty-five miles due south of Valentine.

Gary took me to the bunkhouse, a decrepit, old, two-story structure with a livable basement. A lanky cowboy lounged there. His name was Leonard Paris, and he was from New Mexico. I unpacked my bag and hung my few clothes on a wire stretched across a corner of the room. That night I slept in the bed that would be mine for the next five months.

The next day I called my sister Rachel back in Bloomfield. She taught at one of the two Amish schools there, and each schoolhouse had a community phone. I called her collect and told her where I was. We chatted. She spoke carefully, choosing her words. She said things weren't good at home. The community was abuzz with shock, and my parents were taking it pretty hard.

Years later, she told me that Dad had refused to pay for my collect call. He said she had accepted it, so it was her responsibility. To me, that's a strange and puzzling thing. I had called to let her know where I was and that I was okay. Surely it was worth the cost of the call to Dad, to know that. But he refused to pay, so she paid from her meager teacher's salary. I still owe her for that.

The first few days and weeks at the ranch were a blur. The trauma of leaving so abruptly, so secretively, was washed away by the excitement of my new surroundings. I was rough, uncouth, and raw, fresh from the primitive Amish life that had been the only one I'd ever known. I was eager, but quite naive. A remote ranch in the sand hills of northern Nebraska was probably about as ideal a place as any for my first transition to English life.

In the next few weeks, I acclimated to my surroundings. Leonard Paris was an amiable fellow. He immediately took me under his wing and very patiently taught me the things I didn't know. He was rough around the edges, but he was a gentleman.

He didn't swear much, and he always said please and thank you at the table during our shared meals with Gary's family. I watched and learned and emulated.

I quickly adapted to the ranch work and the brutal schedule. Calving season had just begun, and we had to get up every morning at two or so to check for problem births. Then it was back to bed for a few more hours of sleep before getting up at six for the real day's work.

Leonard regaled me with tall tales of New Mexico and his father's ranch there. He was a true horseman, born to the saddle. His favorite phrase, after telling a tale, was "We have more fun than people."

Gradually, I settled into the rhythm of English life. We worked from dawn to dark. I was used to working, so that was no problem. I just wasn't used to being on my own. But I was learning. And it wasn't as if I could get into much trouble on the ranch.

My pay was room and board and a hundred bucks a week. Four hundred a month. Not a lot, even back then. I was fed well and worked hard. In many ways, it wasn't that much different from what I was used to back home.

Of course, I had to learn to drive a truck—an old green and white 1972 Chevy. I had never driven a truck before, or any other motor vehicle for that matter. Leonard carefully coached me and allowed me to drive from the bunkhouse to the main house for meals. Within days I was confident and comfortable behind the wheel.

The first month passed, and payday approached. And boy, did I ever have places to put that money. I needed a new pair of cowboy boots and a real cowboy hat. I also needed some shirts, more jeans, and maybe a real belt buckle with a horse or a bull or some such appropriate cowboy icon.

That Friday, Robert, the head of the investment group from

Kansas that ran the ranch, stopped by with our paychecks. It was a gray, cloudy day. Robert handed Gary his check, then Leonard his. Then he turned to me.

"Here you are, first paycheck," he said.

"Thank you, sir," I replied, taking it from him.

His eyes glinted mischievously. "It's a nice check," he said. "How would you like to double it?"

I stared at him, uncomprehendingly.

"We'll flip a coin," he continued. "Double or nothing."

He would have done it too. I considered his proposition for about two seconds. I held the slip of paper in my hands and looked at it. My first paycheck. Four hundred bucks. A small fortune for me. I could double it. Or I could end up with nothing.

"Nope," I answered. "Don't wanna do that. I can't afford to lose this."

They all laughed, as did I. Many times since, I've wondered what would have happened if I had taken him up on it. Knowing my luck, I would have remained penniless for another month.

Soon after that, Leonard, who had come to Valentine from the huge feedlots in Kansas as temporary help, returned to his old job. As he left, we shook hands, and he smiled and said he hoped we would run into each other again. I was sure we would. Of course, we never did. He left me with his patented saying, "Remember, we have more fun than people."

Leonard was replaced by a cowboy a year younger than me. A local tough named Allen Hazen. At sixteen, Allen's reputation as a first-rate cowboy and a hard drinker was already well established throughout the Valentine area. He smiled at me with a loopy grin and took it upon himself to coach me throughout my short-lived career as a cowboy.

Up until now, I had not socialized much in Valentine because I didn't know anyone in the area. Gary had introduced me to the neighbors, and everyone was friendly, but I had no social life. And that was okay for a while. I saved a few bucks and bought the basic necessities. But that all changed after Allen arrived.

On his first Saturday night at the ranch, we quit a bit early, cleaned up, slicked up in nice clothes—or at least the nicest ones in my meager closet—and drove to Valentine in his old Ford pickup.

Allen knew all the local kids, and he was quite the stud. The girls loved him. By hanging around him, I soon got to know many of the town kids. On Saturday nights, we hung around partying until the morning hours. I usually drove the thirty-five miles back to the ranch, while Allen slept soundly on the seat beside me in a comfortable drunken stupor.

Life on the ranch had gotten increasingly interesting. While I was perfectly comfortable herding cattle, tending sick cows, and mending fences, I clearly had a lot to learn when it came to socializing.

• • •

Meanwhile, back in Bloomfield, my buddies were continuing in their wild and wicked ways. They called me sometimes, usually on a Sunday morning. Back then, it cost much less to call on Sundays, so that's when they contacted me. They filled me in on the latest, and after a time, I began to feel a tinge of homesickness. I missed them. And I missed my family. But not enough to lure me back.

After I gave Rachel my mailing address, the letters started flowing in—from Mom and, of course, from Dad. Mom wrote from a broken heart. Told me she missed me and wanted me to come home. Dad wrote masterfully, laying on every guilt trip he could devise. Of course they weren't perfect as parents, he wrote.

But they did the best they knew. He had hoped his sons would be happy and settled in Bloomfield. Now I had left, and that was a big disappointment to him and Mom.

And always, he waxed poetic about my spiritual state. I had chosen a path of wickedness. What if I were killed in an accident? Where would I go? How would I fare when I faced the judgment seat? And so on and so on.

I believed that what he said was true—that I had left the protection of the Amish fold and was as good as lost. That there was no hope for me, should I die. That there would never be any chance of salvation outside the Amish church.

That's what he wrote, and that's what I believed. The fires of hell awaited me. That was a fact I never even tried to dispute. But despite that knowledge, I had chosen to leave. And despite that heavy mental burden, I really did not want to return.

My father knew how to write in a way that always cast a cloud of gloom, even on the sunniest day. But I tried hard to shake it off.

I rarely, if ever, wrote back.

Then one Sunday morning, while I was enjoying a rare hour of sleeping in, Gary clattered into the bunkhouse, hollering for me. There was a phone call for me back at the house. I stumbled from the bed, bleary eyed, and got dressed. Gary said the caller would call back in fifteen minutes, so we drove to the house, and I waited. Then the phone rang. It was Vern Herschberger, one of the gang of six in Bloomfield. He had left home early that morning and was at the bus station in Ottumwa. He was heading out to join me.

He arrived the next day, and instantly landed a job at a neighboring ranch about six miles away. A few weeks later, Mervin Gingerich and my best friend, Marvin Yutzy, arrived. By now, the Amish boys from Bloomfield were causing quite a stir among the local ranchers. Gary made his rounds and bragged loudly about how hard we could work. They all wanted a piece of us. Mervin and Marvin landed jobs the day they stepped off the bus. A week or two after that, the last of the six—Willis Herschberger and Rudy Yutzy—arrived. And just like that, there we all were—all six of us—in a radius of about twenty miles, working as cowboys in the sand hills south of Valentine, Nebraska.

It had been a month or two since I'd seen any of them, and I was thrilled to talk to them and hear the news from Bloomfield. As it turned out, things were about as bad as they'd been when I left—maybe even worse.

Our exodus caused a huge uproar in Bloomfield. Five families were affected. Five families left in shock, absorbing the sudden loss, the abrupt disappearance of certain sons. Five sets of parents, including Bishop George, whose son Mervin had left with his buddies. Tongues wagged. The community staggered from the shock and the shame of losing so many of its young sons to the world.

And people in the older communities from which the Bloomfield families had emigrated sadly and dramatically shook their heads. *See how it goes when you move to an untested place like Bloomfield? It's no better than the place you left.*

The Aylmer people, too, I'm sure, smirked silently. *David Wagler moved far away for the sake of his sons, and now look at how they repay him. Better he had stayed in Aylmer and confronted the problems there instead of uprooting his family in such a futile move.*

As for our little gang of six, well, we had done it. Done what we had claimed we could do, back there in the safety of our Amish world. Many Amish kids threaten to leave and never do. They never have the nerve or the guts to go. We did, and no one could ever take that away from us. We were far away, safe in another world. Safe and free.

15

WE QUICKLY SETTLED INTO THE COWBOY LIFE, though the reality was a far cry from my idealized childhood perceptions of it. It was tough work, with long and dreary hours. We rode the range for days on end, herding cattle. Within two months, I was walking bowlegged—and not because I wanted to. Even when everything else was done, there were always endless miles of old, rusty fences to repair. Sometimes Allen and I worked together, and sometimes I went alone, driving the fence rows in an old four-wheel-drive pickup loaded with fencing tools and rolls of barbed wire.

It's a harsh and desolate land, the sand hills of north central Nebraska. Remote and empty, and brutally lonely. The people who live there and scratch a living from the land are tough and hard. They have to be to survive and keep their sanity. It takes many acres of sand hills to sustain one cow for one year, but the very desolation, the emptiness, is a thing of beauty, too. The hills are alive with mule deer, jackrabbits as large as dogs, and coyotes.

And, of course, cattle. On many a day I worked alone, sometimes riding miles through vast empty stretches to retrieve a stray
bull or a few cows.

In late May and early June, it was branding time, and the
ranchers all got together and helped one another, kind of like the
Amish do with their threshing. We loaded the trailer with our
horses and headed out, arriving shortly after daybreak. All the
cows with calves were corralled and ready. Amid much frantic
bawling from their mothers, the calves were then separated, roped
by their hind legs, and unceremoniously dragged to where the
brands were heating on a fire.

Two cowboys grabbed a calf and stretched it out, helpless, on
the ground, while a third approached with the red-hot branding
iron and applied it to the calf's rump. Once branded, all the calves
were vaccinated, and the bull calves were castrated.

The air was filled with smoke, the smell of burning flesh, the
sound of crying calves and bawling cows, and the riotous shouts
of the cowboys. It was all quite exciting. Usually by noon or a bit
later, the task was done, and we all assembled at the ranch house
for the noon meal. After the meal, we sat around outside, and a
bottle of whiskey was passed from man to man. Any cowboy was
free to take a few swigs. It was an exciting time for the six of us.
We were young—kids, really. At sixteen, Rudy was the youngest. Willis was the oldest at eighteen. He was the only legal adult
among us all. Such a thing would probably be impossible, not to
mention illegal, today, to hire minors to work a man's job. Back
in 1979, though, life was a bit less complicated.

We wore jeans and Western shirts and cowboy hats, and we
felt cool. That summer I began smoking cigarettes for real, a
habit that would stay with me, off and on, for almost ten years.
From what I'd seen and read, the ideal cowboy smoked, so I did

too—filterless Camels, the real deal. In my mind, I can still taste them—not an altogether unpleasant memory.

On Saturday nights, we all hit the town. Allen and I usually met the others there, and we would all hang out at the drive-in movie theater, still a staple of small towns back then. That's where all the action was. Teenagers converged every Saturday night and hung out, drinking beer and socializing.

We got to know the fairer sex too. I'd never had much to do with girls in my seventeen years. Not that Bloomfield lacked girls—even beautiful ones—but they were mostly prim and proper. And unapproachable, we felt. Plus, we were actually pretty shy when it came to such things.

The painted, pretty town girls of Valentine seemed like goddesses to us, visions of splendor and worldliness. They were bold, aggressive, and available.

Late one muggy Saturday night, in the summer of 1979, I kissed a girl for the first time. She'd been around. I had not. I still remember her name.

We saw and lived all the things we'd never seen or done—parties, drinking, and dancing on the large hardwood floor to the fiddle and guitars of some two-bit country band at the Norton Dance Hall, an old converted barn out in the country. We heard the arguments and saw the fistfights triggered by the cowboys' sensitive code of honor, which is quick to take offense at the slightest insult, real or perceived.

One night, outside the dance hall, one of our townie buddies tangled with a cowboy from the range. One had said something offensive to the other, and without delay, they faced off and began whacking merrily at each other. The townie's friends and the cowboy's friends hovered close but did not interfere. Had anyone stepped in to help one or the other, a general melee would have ensued. But no one did.

The townie got the worst of it by far. He was beaten and pitched around like a rag until his face was a pulpy and bloody mess. And then, after a few minutes, it was over. The townie's friends helped him up and took him away. Everyone else headed back inside to dance and socialize.

It's a wonder that none of us, the six from Bloomfield, got beaten up. Maybe it was the fact that anyone could glance at us and instantly know we were innocent rubes from another place. Or maybe it was that the real cowboys viewed us with bemused condescension. Whatever the reason, all of us passed through our Valentine days unscathed.

Come Sunday, we always returned to our jobs, broke and hungover, then got up early the next day and slaved in the hot summer sun. We told ourselves we were in the real world and making it. And we were. But we weren't getting ahead. Work, party, drink, blow your money, then go back and do it all over again.

By late summer, the thrill was gone in more ways than one. Gary, the jovial ranch manager with the great booming laugh, turned out to be a hard-driving, volatile man with a fiery temper. He was tough, worked like a maniac, and demanded the same from us. Not that there's anything wrong with that. But on the slightest provocation, his mean streak would surface like a shark from the waters. We never came to blows, he and I, but we got close a few times during sporadic in-your-face shouting and swearing matches. We always patched things up, but I never forgot.

By late August, I was ready to get out of Valentine. I was sick of ranch life, and to be honest, memories of home tugged at me. I missed the security and stability of it—the quiet life, the old Bloomfield haunts, and my family.

And therein lies the paradox that would haunt me for almost ten years: the tug-of-war between two worlds. A world of freedom versus a world of stability and family. A world of dreams versus a world of tradition. And wherever I resided at any given moment, trudging through the tough slog of daily life, the world I had left called me back from the one I inhabited. It was a brutal thing in so many ways, and I seemed helpless to combat it. Torn emotionally, moving back and forth, always following the siren's call to lush and distant fields of peace that seemed so real but, like shimmering mirages in the desert, always faded away when I approached them.

Before heading back home, Mervin Gingerich and I decided to take a two-week trip on Greyhound. After fourteen days of traveling—through Wyoming, the empty beautiful stretches of Utah, into California, to New Orleans, and back north—we ended up in Ottumwa one Sunday evening, flat broke. We didn't have a dime between us—just a couple of candy bars and half a pack of cigarettes.

We called an English friend from Bloomfield to pick us up and take us home. Around dusk that evening, we pulled into the long drive that led to my family's farm. I stepped out, lugging my faithful black duffel bag—the same one I'd carried down the lane the previous April. Slowly I walked up the concrete walkway to the house.

Mom met me at the door. She smiled in welcome. My younger siblings, Rhoda and Nathan, clamored about excitedly. The older children were all at the Sunday evening singing. Dad was in his little office, typing away. Eventually, he heard the bustle of excitement and walked out to the living room. By then I was downstairs in the bedroom, unpacking.

As I walked back upstairs to the kitchen, I met him on the landing, halfway up. We paused in the semidarkness and faced each other.

"Ira." It was a half question, tinged with disbelief.

"Hello, Dad," I said.

"You came home." His voice quivered slightly.

"Yep," I grunted.

I walked on up. And he walked out. There just wasn't a whole lot to say.

• • •

I didn't particularly have my pulse on Bloomfield's gossip lines at the time, but I'm sure the news swept through the community very quickly. Two of the six outlaws had returned. Ira and Mervin.

We were back inside the box and the perceived safety of that world. Back to what we had left, not that long ago, in search of adventure and freedom. Back to the world of horse and buggy, barn-door pants, and galluses—and a whole lot more. The world of home. We settled in uneasily.

Those first few weeks were strange, almost surreal. We were forced back into the slow pace of Amish life. No more trucks. No more running to town on Saturday nights. No more hanging out with the English girls of Valentine. We worked on the farm. Attended church on Sundays. The singings on Sunday nights. The other youth welcomed us. Whatever they thought inside, they were friendly enough.

But home, I soon discovered, wasn't quite the same. It would never be again. And I could never truly return, even as I participated in the community, its life and customs. On one hand, I loved the camaraderie, the feeling of belonging. But, wherever I was at any given moment, the grass always seemed greener on the other side. When I was home, I heard the siren's song of the outside world. I had followed that song into that outside world until the memories of home had tugged at my heart and pulled me back.

Always I grasped, with tenacious grip, at the anticipation of something rare, something great and grand and fine. Something beyond.

I grasped for tomorrow, with its visions of splendor and a shining city. I dreamed of adventures in strange and distant lands, and of a brighter future of happiness and contentment that always seemed to be just beyond the tip of my outstretched hand.

I would find it tomorrow. Always tomorrow.

16

MERVIN GINGERICH AND I slowly settled into the rhythm of what passed for normal life in Bloomfield. But I had a sinking feeling in my stomach, a sense of quiet desperation. I didn't think about it much, but it was there. Desperation and tinges of despair. Deep down. Way deep down.

I went through the motions. I worked hard that fall on the farm. Harvesting corn. Plowing the fields behind jangling teams of horses. The world I had inhabited a few short months before in Valentine now seemed far away, in both miles and time.

On the surface, I'm sure I seemed like a normal eighteen-year-old kid, with normal teenage issues. And I fooled most of the people, most of the time. I smiled and laughed, at least in public.

Mervin seemed to genuinely settle in and settle down, and we still hung out on Sundays. Meanwhile, our four buddies remained in Valentine, doing who knows what. I thought of them a lot.

And then, sometime in September, word trickled in and quickly spread through the youth grapevine—the four remaining rebels were coming back home.

They returned a few weeks later—a group of four swash-buckling kids, mildly subdued but still defiant, sporting long hair and worldly haircuts. By then I had reverted to the upended-bowl haircut.

One night during the first week after their return, I hitched up my horse and buggy after supper and rattled over the five miles of gravel roads to my friend Marvin Yutzy's place. He emerged from the house, grinning. We shook hands and then sat on the buggy and talked.

"We've been pretty calm since we got back, me and Mervin," I said. "I'm not sure what's going on, but I think Mervin will probably join the church next spring. He seems to be heading in that direction."

Neither Marvin nor I were particularly inclined to join church quite yet. I had just turned eighteen. And he was about to, in December. In the end, we both thought it would be best to wait another year and see what developed.

Nevertheless, we were back—the six of us. Back safely in the fold. But somehow, after the Valentine experience, we never quite connected like before. Sure, we still hung out. Rehashed our experiences. Told war stories. Got together with the other youth on Sunday nights, and one night a week we played hockey out on the iced-over ponds. But it just wasn't the same.

January passed.

February.

Then March arrived. And with it came a huge event. The wedding of my sister Rachel. She had been dating Lester Yutzy, Rudy's older brother, for a couple of years, and they had made plans to marry that month—March 6, 1980. The wedding was to be held at our home.

The last time we had held a wedding at our house was my sister Naomi's wedding to Alvin Yutzy, an intense man a few years her junior, in the spring of 1978.

And I faintly remember my oldest sister, Rosemary's, wedding in Aylmer. I was four or five years old. I recall much commotion about the house, nothing at all of the service itself, and boxes and boxes of hot dogs Dad had bought for the noon meal. Red boxes, with a picture of a chef waving a spatula. Hot dogs were a rare treat, entirely suitable for a wedding feast.

There weren't many weddings in Aylmer when we lived there, because the church fathers had dictated some very stringent rules on dating. For example, when a couple started dating, they could see each other only once a month, or every four weeks. Then, when things got really serious (expressions of love, talk of marriage, and so on) and they were "going steady," they could increase that schedule to one date every two weeks. (Love made the days fly, I'm sure.)

And the couple had better not get caught sneaking around or even looking at each other between dates. Anyone caught in such verboten activity could expect a prompt visit from the deacon, a grizzled, imposing man. And he wouldn't be there to chat about the weather, either. At least not for long.

I don't know if the Aylmer church fathers thought the end of the world was imminent and procreation was therefore unnecessary, or what. But that's the way it was. Talk about regressive conservatism.

After we moved to Bloomfield, we discovered that dating couples there could see each other every week. We felt very liberated. Or at least my siblings did. Within a span of about six or seven years, five of them got married.

Needless to say, over the years I took part in many weddings. My favorite job was waiting on tables for the noon meal. As a table waiter, you got to putz around getting ready in the morning, and you could leave the wedding service immediately after the vows to go and prepare to serve the meal. All told, a table waiter might have to sit for maybe an hour as opposed to the full three or four hours the regular guests had to sit quietly on those backless benches.

Being a witness attendant, or "Nava Hocca," was the least favorite job. The wedding couple had two sets of such attendants with them all day. It was considered the higher honor, to be Nava Hocca, but it was vastly more tiresome and boring. More than once I fell sound asleep sitting straight up with no support to lean against. (Try it sometime. It's hard to do.)

Anyway, an Amish wedding is an all-day affair. The morning service begins at nine or nine thirty. A good preacher can make the time pass relatively unnoticed, but chances are that the preacher will be as boring as chalk on a blackboard and drone on and on.

Few things in life are more irritating than a boring Amish preacher who likes the sound of his own voice and doesn't pay attention to the time. And there are plenty out there. Sometimes the hands on the clock seem to stand still, or even go backward, resulting in what feels like an endless day and restless guests.

Another major irritant often occurs when the deacon, whose only job is to read a bit of Scripture, forgets his calling and decides to deliver an impromptu sermon of his own. Some deacons have been known to ramble on for up to twenty minutes. Whatever good they might imagine results from their words disappears in the hostile gaze of seething listeners whose only wish is that the speaker read the assigned verses and sit down.

Everyone is greatly relieved when the bishop instructs the couple—if they still feel as they did that morning—to tread before him. They then rise, walk carefully up to him, and stand in front of him. At this moment, the Nava Hocca stand at attention.

This is their official purpose, to "witness" the ceremony. After a prayer, the bishop administers the vows, places the couple's hands together, and pronounces them man and wife. Then they return to their seats as such. From that moment until death.

After we turned sixteen and joined the youth, or Rumspringa, we looked forward to weddings because we could ask a girl to the table for the evening meal and singing. This was not considered a date, and the girls rarely turned down an invitation. It always created a buzz, to see which guy would escort which girl. More than a few married couples began their relationship at the evening wedding feast of someone else.

That's how it goes at Amish weddings, with a few minor variations, depending on the community where it's all coming down.

Before Rachel's wedding, we spent weeks getting ready. Junk machinery that had been littering the yard for months, sometimes years, was pulled up the hill behind the woods and out of sight. All the barns were cleaned. And the house, well, the house was scoured from bottom to top, scrubbed, wiped, mopped, and cleaned until it was glistening. It was a busy, frantic time, but when the big day arrived, we would be ready.

It's an important event, a wedding. Simple, but important. There are many relatives to invite, and in our case, many guests from Aylmer. We hoped they would come so we could show them how progressive a Bloomfield wedding service was.

Guests began trickling in the day before the wedding in large passenger vans loaded with people and luggage. The exceptions were, of course, the Aylmer people, who came by bus or train, as they were not allowed to hire a van driver for overnight trips, due to the dictates of preacher Elmo Stoll's regime.

We were happy and excited to see everyone. And, of course, we were busy preparing, right up to the last minute.

Then the day was upon us. The benches for the service were

set up in Joseph's house, and the tables for food were set up in our house. Dad walked about importantly. Mom beamed and fussed and worried. And I was a table waiter. Looking back, it was a plain affair, but to us, it was huge. Things seemed to be going very well for the Wagler family in Bloomfield.

I don't have a lot of specific memories of that day, other than the fact that Rachel and Lester were properly married, and a large crowd of guests assembled to witness and celebrate the event.

I do have vivid memories of what came down the day *after* the wedding.

17

AFTER THE WEDDING, my uncle and his family stayed for a day or two to visit. His son Eli was a year older than I was, and we had always been close friends. On those rare times we got together, everyone could be sure of one thing—somehow, someway, we *would* get into trouble. When we were kids, it was usually just harmless pranks: passing around comic books and bragging about which brand of car was the best. (Eli was a Ford man. I liked Chevy.) And a few other verboten things, things so trite they actually escape my memory. As I said, absolutely harmless. But as we grew, we graduated to more serious offenses, like smoking, drinking, and buying radios. Now we were adults. I was eighteen. Eli was nineteen. And we were about to graduate to the big leagues of wild Amish living.

The morning after the wedding, Eli and I announced that we were hitchhiking up to Ottumwa, twenty-five miles northeast. The adults frowned. My dad strongly discouraged us from going, but we ignored him, and shortly after breakfast, we headed up to Highway 2, stood beside the road, and thumbed a ride into Bloomfield. I knew some English people there, and one of them readily agreed to take us up to Ottumwa, fifteen miles north.

Once there, we decided to pool our meager funds and look for a used car to buy. After all these years, I'm not sure whose idea it was, or when it first came up. I don't remember who suggested it. Might have been a mutual thing we both conceived at the same instant. I know that in the ensuing months, my family blamed Eli, and his family blamed me. But I'll take the full blame right now, just to clear up that ancient tiff. It was probably my idea anyway, being more experienced in leaving and all.

We had probably five hundred dollars between us. So we headed to a car lot along Highway 34, just east of the city. It was a dreary, rainy day, and we arrived on the used-car lot dressed in Amish barn-door pants with galluses and plain denim jackets—all homemade, of course. The smarmy salesman greeted us with a shifty smile. Could he help us? Plainly, he doubted that he could.

We were just looking for a used car, we told him. Might be in the market for a purchase. His eyes immediately perked up. We told him we had about three or four hundred dollars to spend, and he led us to the back of the lot to an old two-door Dodge painted an ugly avocado green. I don't remember the model name, but it was built in 1972. The salesman claimed it was a good old car.

"Heck, it only has seventy-five thousand miles on it," he said. "This car will run and run, way over a hundred thousand miles."

"How much?" we asked, trying to act uninterested.

"Four hundred dollars."

What a coincidence—almost exactly what we had to spend.

"Could we take it for a test drive?"

"Of course."

And, of course, the car wouldn't start. Dead battery. So the salesman dragged an old black charger from the jumbled mess in his garage and hooked it up. Then he took us inside to draw up the paperwork.

Looking back, if either Eli or I had expressed even the slightest reservation—if either of us had had the sense to say, "Wait a minute. Let's think this through. Should we really be doing this?"—we would have backed out. But we didn't. That's what always happened when we got together. We'd step out on some bold adventure, and neither of us wanted to be the first to break. And so we hurtled on, straight over the cliff's edge.

By the time the salesman got the car started and drew up the paperwork, it was getting late. We handed him a fistful of crumpled twenties, and after carefully counting it, he slapped a license plate on our new car, and that was that. So, without a shred of insurance, we edged the car out of the parking lot and onto the highway.

So far, so good. But now what? We hadn't planned ahead at all. What to do? Head back home? That wouldn't work. We had a car; we couldn't go back home. Park it somewhere, maybe, at my English friends' place in Bloomfield? That would have actually made some sense. But on that day, we were devoid of sense. After the excitement of buying a car, we couldn't imagine heading back to my house. We wouldn't be able to keep our secret. Besides, we wanted to hit the road in our new car. Head out into the big, wide world.

We decided to head south on Highway 63, into Missouri, toward Eli's home in Marshfield, three hundred miles away. So off we went, through the darkness, with only the clothes on our backs, a few bucks, and an old green Dodge with no insurance.

We headed south through the darkness, and the old Dodge hummed along. It seemed like a decent car, and it actually turned out to be. We drove through horrible weather as biting rain turned to sleet, icing the roads. Around the Missouri line, I almost lost control. The car skidded violently from one side of the road to the other while I frantically cranked the wheel. We very nearly landed in the ditch. After regaining control, we crept along until we came to a motel and restaurant, where we pulled in, booked a room, and ate.

We had no bags, no extra clothes, nothing. By the seat of our pants, and with no forethought, we were leaving home.

We sent no word to our families to let them know our plans or where we were. That was the cruelest part of that black and wicked day. Back home, as the afternoon began inching into evening, I'm sure the folks became increasingly restless and worried. Eli and I had our reputations; our families probably had no doubt that we were involved in some sort of mischief. Years later, my father told me how frantic and worried they were when we didn't show up. His voice heavy with emotion, he spoke of how his younger sister, Eli's mom, stood in the rain at the end of the walks and peered into the darkness. To the south, out our long lane toward the road, she strained and looked and called her son's name. There was no answer. Only the mocking sound of rain and the wind slashing through the trees. And intermittent silence.

Eventually she gave up and straggled back into the house, soaked and chilled to the bone. No one ate supper that night. And sleep was far away and fleeting—a hopeless thing—as the two families, Eli's and mine, sat there and wondered if they'd ever see us alive again.

At the motel, twenty-five miles south of our worried, frantic families, we slept soundly. The next morning dawned, a nice clear day. The roads were good. But our green machine wouldn't start. Dead battery. The smarmy salesman had taken us. After purchasing a new battery at a nearby garage, we headed south again, down Route 63, with not a care in the world, except that we were running low on funds.

We reached Eli's home turf late that afternoon. Still no plan for how we would survive or where we would live.

We scrabbled some odd jobs here and there for money on which to live. Eli claimed to own some calves on his father's farm, and at night, we would sneak in and grab a few from the pasture, tie them up, place them in the trunk of the old green Dodge, and sell them to a local English farmer. Technically, of course, the calves didn't really belong to Eli, but to his dad. I knew it and he knew it. But we took them anyway, and sold them. We were flat out stealing. Each time, the money kept us going for a few more days.

The news flashed three hundred miles back to Bloomfield about what the wicked boys were up to these days. (Or down to.) People clucked their tongues and shook their heads, and wondered aloud if we'd land in jail.

We never found a fixed place to stay in Marshfield. Instead, we slept in seedy hotels, and sometimes in the car. But we hadn't quite reached our low point—yet.

After a few weeks, we decided to head back to Bloomfield in search of greener pastures. I'm not sure what we wanted there or why we went. I guess I just longed for my old stomping grounds. I missed my friends and wondered how they were. Eli and I were pretty much social outcasts. Outlaws. Drifters. With only each other for support. And that got a little tricky, in our heads. We argued and fussed sometimes. The stress of our situation went far deeper and affected us far more than either of us could possibly recognize or comprehend.

We needed to hear words of affirmation. Words that would never come from anyone in our families. But we might hear them from my friends back in Bloomfield. And so, lonely and longing for something we did not have and could not find, we returned.

Back in Bloomfield, we skulked about the community, hooked

up with my old buddies, and ran around at night. We had no place to call our own and often slept in the car, huddling under blankets to fend off the night chill. We lived from day to day, sometimes from hour to hour, never really sure what we were doing next.

Regardless of how bad conditions might have been at home, they weren't as bad as that. But home was off limits to us now, after the stunt we'd pulled, leaving as we did with no word or warning. Besides, Dad had an ironclad rule: No son of his could live in his home and own a car. The line was clear. And I had crossed it. So the thought of returning didn't even enter my mind, even though my "home" was only a few miles away.

After a week or so, our funds depleted, we decided to head to Arthur, Illinois. Willis Herschberger, one of the old gang of six, agreed to go with us. He came from Arthur and knew the place and the people. Maybe we'd be able to find work there.

And therein lies another paradox—Amish kids who leave and yet don't. Instead, they hang around their own communities or, as in our case, head for larger communities where their language is spoken. Where there is some sense of familiarity, even though they remain outside the boundaries of acceptance in the Amish culture.

Some invisible force draws them, as it drew us. Some sense of belonging, even outside the lines. And some sense of security, a sense that if everything fell apart, at least we would be among our own people. That is a strange thing, one that cannot really be defined.

We planned to leave the next Sunday morning. I don't remember who had the idea, and it doesn't matter, but before heading out, we decided to tour past Amish places. We knew everyone was in church, and we figured we could find a place to steal some gas. The Amish wouldn't call the cops. We knew that. In our clouded minds, it actually seemed like a good idea at the time.

We cruised slowly through the neighborhood. Found where church was that day and then headed to the other end of the settlement, to Jake Schwartz's farm, up on the north side. That would be the place, we figured. There were no close neighbors with prying eyes. We approached and pulled in cautiously, just in case someone was home.

No one was. We located the gas barrel behind a shed and backed up the car. Then we discovered a lock on the nozzle of the hose. One of us—I can't remember who—ran to Jake's shop and returned with a hacksaw. We made short work of the padlock and threw it into the bushes. Then I removed the nozzle and began to fill the tank. We stood nervously, waiting for the tank to fill.

Then Willis looked out toward the road. "Uh-oh," he muttered.

I looked up from where I was filling the tank.

Out by the road, a pickup truck had pulled up and stopped. A neighbor. He had seen us and come to check on what was happening. The three of us stood there, momentarily frozen, our hearts tripping fast. We were discovered. Caught. Maybe the neighbor had already called the cops.

I snapped the nozzle back onto the tank. Shut the gas tank lid on our car. We scurried around frantically. Eli and Willis both leaped into the car. One of them went for the passenger's seat, the other into the backseat. That left me to drive. Frantically, I circled the car. "I don't want to drive! I don't want to drive!" I hollered.

Eli and Willis were having none of it. "Get in and drive!" they shouted back in unison.

And so I did. We barreled out the lane and onto the road, gravel spitting behind us. *Come on, old green Dodge, don't let us down now.* I turned right, shot past the waiting pickup, and roared full speed down the road.

It was a time before cell phones, or we would have been caught dead to rights. I turned the car south, fishtailing a bit on the gravel, then onto the paved highway. We flew toward Route 63, the pickup in hot pursuit.

Eli and Willis kept a close eye on the pickup right on our tail, the man inside motioning us to pull over. I paid no attention, just focused on the road ahead. I kept driving, right through the community, past several Amish homes, and up to Route 63 South. More often than not, a cop would be sitting at the intersection there. If one was there today, we would go to jail for sure.

Then, a stroke of luck—no cop. I turned south and floored the accelerator. The old green Dodge rocketed along, with three desperate, panic-stricken boys inside. After ten miles or so we approached the Missouri line, and the pickup, up to now riding our tail, slowed and stopped, then turned around and headed back north. I slowed the car to the speed limit, and we all sagged in our seats, breathing huge sighs of relief as our heartbeats slowed to normal speed. We had escaped.

After an experience like that, there isn't a whole lot to say. We actually shook it off as just another event in the normal course of things. That's how screwed up we were. Of course, back in Bloomfield our reputations took another serious hit as the story— greatly embellished, I'm sure—made its inevitable rounds.

We were officially outlaws.

Renegades.

Wild Amish youth.

And we were lost. We knew it—at least I did. We didn't talk about it, but we knew that if something happened and we were killed, we would straightaway enter the fiery pits of hell and burn forever because we had left the safety of the protective box. We had scorned our birthright. Left the Amish. If we died, the punishment for such blasphemy would be more severe than we could possibly imagine. We knew that, beyond any shadow of a doubt. But we plunged on anyway. Grimly focused on what we felt we had to do. If God struck us down, well, then, so be it.

It takes a desperate mind to be willing to take such risks against such eternal consequences. But we were beyond desperate.

• • •

For the next two months, Eli and I bummed along. Our cash flow improved some, but mostly the times were lean. We had a saying, "If we're too broke to buy a pack of smokes, we're truly broke." We reached that point a time or two. But mostly, we survived okay.

We worked at odd jobs around the Arthur area for a month, hanging out with Willis and his buddies. Then Eli and I decided to pull up and go to Daviess County. We didn't know many people there, but at least my brother Jesse lived there. We said good-bye to Willis and left Arthur, heading south and east.

We found Jesse's place and showed up at the door of his trailer home. Although surprised and not all that pleased to see us, he gave us shelter and some work, cleaning up an old burned-out house site he had bought in a nearby village. We meandered along for several weeks with no long-term plans, and everywhere we went, the whispered stories of what we'd done back in Bloomfield preceded us.

On the weekends we ran with the Daviess Amish youth. We made a lot of friends because we had a car. Many a time, the old green Dodge creaked along on the narrow gravel roads, loaded to the gills with rowdy Amish youth.

After another month had passed, we realized that we were pretty much spinning our wheels. We didn't want to face it, but it was becoming clearer with each passing day—our options were running out. We could continue down this bleak and desolate road, struggling for survival. Struggling for our daily bread. Or we could return to our homes, where at least we would be warm and sheltered and fed. Mine in Bloomfield and Eli's in Marshfield. Initially, we recoiled from the thought. But gradually the conditions of our surroundings closed in. We had no support. Not from any source, not from anywhere. No prospects for a brighter future out here, outside the box. Our only option was to go back. Back to our respective homes. Back again, to the Amish life. We'd had a lot of excitement on this little run. We'd seen and done things we'd never seen or done before. It was time for some rest and some stability.

Eli left by bus one morning for his home in Marshfield, and I drove home to Bloomfield. It's impossible to describe that feeling, of approaching home after an infamous extended foray like that. Had I been honest with myself, I would have admitted that I did not want to go. But I was not honest with myself. Besides, the economic conditions of surviving out there were tough.

And thus ended my second desperate flight from home.

18

I RETURNED LATE THAT SATURDAY NIGHT, AFTER DARK. Pulled the car right up the drive and parked. Dad was surprised to see me, as were all the others. I was tired, so tired. But they all welcomed me.

I already knew that Marvin, Rudy, and Mervin had started joining the church a few weeks before. I wondered if it would be too late to join with them. Not because I had suddenly seen the light and turned over a new leaf. Not because I had turned from my sins in a dramatic conversion. But simply because I wanted to be with my buddies.

And so, the very first day after returning home, on that Sunday morning in church as the preachers walked solemnly from the room, I got up with my friends and followed them.

It's an impossible jolt to the mind, the thing I was attempting—running wild, from town to town and state to state for months, then abruptly changing back. And not only that, but changing to the point that I was joining the church. I should have known better than to try. And the church leaders should have known better than to allow me to try.

The effort was doomed from the start.

At least I finally discovered what goes on inside the preachers' conference for baptismal instruction. It's all pretty formal. The applicants, my buddies and I, sat there solemnly as each of the preachers, beginning with the bishop, instructed and admonished us for about five or ten minutes. Nothing unique or personal. They never addressed us directly or spoke our names. They barely even glanced at us. Mostly they spoke pious clichés and vacant generalizations: "We thank the Lord this morning for his blessings. Today, we have much to be thankful for. We have life, and health, and the church to guide us. And this morning, we are thankful that the future of the church will come through young people like all of you. We are so thankful that you have made the choice to come and take instruction and admonishment and be baptized. This is one important step in your lives that you will never regret." And so forth, and so on. And so on.

But their words, although relevant and at least partially true, were devoid of life and passion. After about half an hour, they wrapped it up, and we were dismissed to return to the congregation.

So we went through the motions and waited for the internal revelations. The mental transformation, where all would be clear to us. Where we could see and walk the path our parents wanted for us.

Sadly, it was not to be.

A mental choice, absent real internal change, is no choice at all. We couldn't force ourselves to be something we were not. That just couldn't happen. And it didn't.

Most of the group stayed with it, but Marvin Yutzy and I ran into trouble almost from the start. We weren't quite ready to give it all up, not just yet. And the more we resisted, the harder the preachers crushed their heels on us.

We were closely watched.

And strongly criticized, everything from our attitudes to how we combed our hair. And, of course, the classic gripe—our sideburns were too long. Like countless others before us through the years, we simmered under the pressures. Hung together. Sneaked around. And as the weeks passed, we knew—at least I knew—we could not continue. Marvin might have made it had I not been in the picture. But as my best friend, he remained intensely loyal. Whatever happened, we were in it together.

The preachers saw it coming. So did our parents. They did all they knew to do to stop it (which wasn't a whole lot). They fussed and scolded. Pleaded and threatened. We were deluged from all sides. We should just straighten up and behave. Decide to do right. But their words seemed empty, like so much sound and fury, signifying little of value to us.

And so things continued uneasily for a few months until it all came to a head one Sunday night at the singing.

Church had been at our home that day, and the singing was that night. After supper, we hung out as usual, and as eight o'clock approached, we filed into the living room to sing. Marvin and I sat together, not quite at the back. We were having a merry old time, whispering and laughing between the songs and during the singing. We weren't greatly disruptive, but our actions triggered a furious response from my father.

As we whispered and laughed, I caught sight of him now and then out of the corner of my eye, motioning fiercely. *Be quiet.* We paid no attention.

Finally, he could not take it anymore. During the next song, he got up, walked to the bench in front of us, and motioned people to move aside to make room for him, and plunked down.

If we wouldn't behave, by George, he was going to embarrass us in front of everyone. The song faltered along, and he rocked back and forth on the bench, throwing back his head and roaring loudly, off-key.

We sat frozen in disbelief, too stunned to react. Then, in one motion, we stood and walked out. No one followed. I was so angry that I shook. We hitched up my horse and drove off toward West Grove. Once there, we tied the horse behind Chuck's Café and called some English friends from the pay phone. They came out from Bloomfield and picked us up.

We hung out with them until late, raging against my father. After midnight, one of them took us back.

The next Sunday, we stopped following church. As the others got up and walked after the preachers to receive their instruction, we remained seated.

People stared, but we just sat there, grim and rebellious.

We hung together, the two of us. We were closely watched as evil young men, and we were instant suspects as the source of all things bad that happened in the community.

Late one Sunday night, a few of us were hanging out at the schoolhouse, just horsing around, when one of my buddies who was joining church was somehow pushed into the front screen door. After a choice phrase or two, he proceeded to tear the door right off its hinges. I don't know why. Of course, the next day, shock waves reverberated throughout the community, and Marvin and I were instantly and conveniently blamed, although neither of us had had anything to do with it.

Tongues wagged: "The wild, wicked young boys tore up the schoolhouse." "What will they do next—burn someone's house down?" "How can it be?" "What can be done?" Everyone clucked sadly and dramatically. One young preacher even began spreading the rumor that we had admitted to the damage.

Marvin and I were indignant. Things were getting out of hand. Should we just hunker down, or should we confront the situation head-on? After discussing our options, we got together one night and went to visit the young preacher.

We rattled into his drive and tied up the horse. Although stunned to see us, he greeted us politely enough, if somewhat stiffly. We visited for a brief strained minute about other things. Haying. The weather. Then we bravely plunged into our subject matter. We told him he had been mistaken and that we had not damaged the schoolhouse door. But we did not betray our friend who had done it. The preacher was in a bit of a quandary. He was convinced in his mind that we'd done it, but there we stood, telling him we hadn't.

We were polite, but firm and insistent. And innocent. He stroked his long reddish beard thoughtfully, perhaps trying to imagine how he could incorporate this experience into a fire-and-brimstone sermon the next time he preached. But we remained polite and respectful, giving him nothing about which he could wring his hands over and preach. No shocking behavior, no back talk. After some moments of consideration, he gulped and cleared his throat several times.

Then he said carefully and deliberately, "I can believe it, and I want to believe it, and I will believe it, that you didn't do it." His stern visage did not soften, not even a fraction.

We thanked him and left it at that.

He was true to his word, whether he actually believed us or not. For that one statement, at least, I have always respected him.

19

As I've said, when I look back, I believe Marvin might have stuck it out had I not influenced him. But being the true friend he was, he hung in there with me. Gradually we made our plans to leave once again, saving up a few bucks where we could. I even sold my shotgun for some quick money.

I'm not sure that we would have chosen to leave, had the walls of our world not been closing in around us. I mean, I'd left twice already and returned. Marvin had left once and returned. It's not an easy thing, to pick up, pack up, and head out. And it's not an easy thing to return. Either physically or emotionally. In a sense, I guess, we were acting like bugs on a hot stove top. Moving around instinctively to the edges, where there was less heat. And right then, the heat was on in Bloomfield. It might be less so in, say, Florida.

They all knew we were going, our families, even though we never came out and said so. They could tell. Then one evening, after everyone else had already retired, I got up to get ready for bed. Dad was sitting on the couch, reading *The Budget*. As I walked by him, he cleared his throat, his classic method of triggering a conversation. I stopped and looked at him.

"Ahem." He cleared his throat again. "I have a question for you." He paused. I stood there silently, looking at him.

"Will you be around over the winter and to help with farming in the spring?"

That was it. A simple question. But I was astounded. It was the first time in my life that Dad gave even the slightest indication that I might have a choice in the matter. It was the first time in my memory that such a subject was broached without all the strident admonitions of how I should straighten up, behave myself, and settle down.

I stood there, gaping at him. Speechless. What had gotten into the man? He was asking me if I was going to leave or stay home to help with the farmwork.

In retrospect, I think, it was the first time ever that he spoke to me as a man. Man to man. And that's why I was so surprised. Sad to say, I did not rise to the occasion. I stuttered a bit, hedging. I knew I was leaving. Our plans were firming up every day. It was just a matter of weeks now.

Finally I spoke. "I don't know," I mumbled. It was a lie. Of course I knew. And he knew I knew. I just wasn't brave enough to tell him straight out. I wasn't used to being treated as if I had a thought of my own. Or choices. But he let it go.

"Well, it would be nice if we knew whether or not we'll need to hire some help this spring," he said. Then he turned back to his paper. Still stunned, I went off to bed.

• • •

We left a month or so after that, in January 1981. Again. The third time for me in as many years. My deeds and choices were rapidly cementing my reputation as a hard-core rebel. And yet, through it all, I can honestly say that I harbored little anger in my heart. Some, sure. But mostly sadness. And increasing desperation. Each time I left made it that much harder to imagine ever returning for good.

We left, this time, in the full light of day. No sneaking out at night. No notes under the pillow. And no disappearing during the day without any word or warning. I still remember the heaviness in the house that day. Mom flitted about, not saying a lot, making sure I had some clean clothes packed. I didn't have the heart to tell her that there wasn't much sense packing Amish clothes because where I was going, I wouldn't need them. So I let her pack some in my suitcase. Dad didn't formally say good-bye; instead, he disappeared into his little office to write. Rhoda, my younger sister, chatted amiably, but I could see she was tense and sad. She told me to be careful and gave me a candy bar, a precious treat, to eat on the road. Nathan lurked about somewhere, out of sight. Silent. Watching.

I wasn't particularly joyous; all I wanted was to be out of there. Away from this oppressive place. To new experiences in new lands.

After lunch, one of my English friends drove in with his car. I picked up my bags and walked out. Marvin had found his own way to town. We met in Bloomfield, boarded the bus, and headed south. Our destination, Florida, seemed like a good place, especially during the middle of an Iowa winter.

We traveled to Sarasota, Florida, and the little suburb of Pinecraft, which for decades has been a winter hot spot for vacationing Amish and Mennonite people—and for wild Amish youth. We knew few people when we got there. Even so, we soon found a room and jobs.

Our money was tight, as always. And the first few weeks were tough. During the day, we toiled in the hot Florida sun, mixing mud and slinging heavy concrete blocks on a mason crew. And gradually, as the days and weeks passed, we settled in.

We pooled our funds that summer and bought an old 1971 Mercury Cougar, an old-style powerhouse with a 351 Cleveland engine. Being Amish farm boys, we had no clue what a 351 Cleveland was, but everyone seemed impressed when we bragged about it.

With our own wheels, we were as free as we'd ever been. We worked shirtless in the sun all that summer. Hard, lean, tanned to a deep, deep brown, and impossibly fit, we were in the prime and passion of young adulthood.

And life was pretty good. We lived in a tiny one-room shack, a converted garage behind someone's house. It was truly small, probably twelve by fifteen feet, with a tiny bathroom and shower, a bed in one corner, and a pullout couch. But it was our own. We made friends among Amish youth from other settlements across the land and found they were a good deal like us. On weekends, we partied hard. (This was back when the legal drinking age was still eighteen.) We hung out in bars on Saturday nights until they closed, then drove home, solidly impaired, yet always arriving unscathed. In those bars I imbibed and enjoyed shots of Wild Turkey whiskey for the first time and marveled at the way it made me feel.

One Saturday night that fall, in the Flamingo Bar, located in some faceless strip mall in suburban Sarasota, someone tutored me on the intricacies of the game of football. I'd never understood it before, but that night I saw for the first time what a great and brilliant game it was. On an old color TV on the wall, the New York Jets were playing some other team I don't remember. It was preseason, and the Jets were engineering a furious but futile comeback in the closing minutes. And on the spot I rashly declared myself a Jets fan. It has been a long and mostly dreary journey since that night. But hope springs eternal.

As the weeks trickled by, we did the things that young men did back in those days, and while we didn't necessarily prosper, we survived.

Of course, our survival did not include much thought about the future. Not in any coherent sense. Vaguely, we figured we'd return to Bloomfield. And the Amish church. Someday. And make it work, as we had seen so many others do. As some of our buddies had already done. But there was no set date; in close to the purest sense, we lived from day to day and from week to week. Nothing more than that. It was as if we existed in a mental fog.

I still smoked. Ever since my Nebraska days I had been hooked on tobacco. I couldn't imagine starting a day without that first delicious cigarette. No, it wasn't healthy. But at that age, youth believes it will live forever.

• • •

It was a strange thing, and I don't quite understand it, even today, but when we were out there, living and working in normal society, thoughts of home, the good things— the security, the family, the comforts—somehow always crept in and drew us back. And so it was that year in Florida.

Sometime that fall, probably in September, we both knew that we would be back home in Bloomfield by winter. It didn't seem like a bad thing. We'd been gone for the better part of a year, and we longed for our old haunts, our old friends.

By late October, both of us had returned. This time, we were determined to make it work. This time, we would do it. *This time,* we really meant it.

That vague and distant future, never more than two weeks out, was now upon us. The time had come for us to do what we had seen so many others around us do, including wild youth we had met and befriended in Pinecraft. (A good many of them are settled and married today, with families. Amish.) Now we, too, would walk that path. It was time.

In my head I figured I could make it work. I knew I could. Somehow. But in my heart, well, those were days when promptings from the heart were quashed. Ignored. Buried, somewhere, out there on the edges of my consciousness, where they belonged. So I trudged doggedly onward, determined to endure whatever it took to settle down and remain Amish.

• • •

The preachers greeted us kindly enough when we made known our plans to join church the next spring. As rigid and unbending as the Amish might appear, one thing is true: Any wayward son (or daughter) who returns to the fold of the Amish church is always welcomed, regardless of what he has done in the past. He might be viewed a bit warily, and sure, he has some things to prove. But he is still welcomed, and genuinely so.

Marvin lived in the east district, so we didn't get to join together. Instead, he followed church with a little group of slightly younger youth. By now, my district had ordained its own bishop, our neighbor Henry Hochstedler, who had been a preacher for years. In my district, I took the baptismal instructions with one other young man, Chris Hochstedler. Bishop Henry's son.

Bishop Henry was originally from Arthur, Illinois. He was a kind man, mostly, but pretty set in his ways. A plodding, methodical worker, he kept his little farm impeccably tidy. All his animals were well cared for, his horses fat and gleaming. He milked a few cows and raised a flock of sheep, struggling bravely to pay his bills.

He preached the same way he worked: slowly, methodically, the words rolling effortlessly from his tongue in a rhythmic, lulling flow. As a bishop, he was unexceptional but steady. Under this man, then, I began my second try at joining the Amish church.

For me, the summer was one of deep, quiet desperation. I seemed to be walking down a long, dark hallway with no light at the end. And no end, for that matter. But I was determined this time to stick it out. To go all the way. It would not be an easy road.

From a distance, or from outside, my decision makes no sense. But it made all the sense in the world to me in that moment, to keep slogging on, to walk the road that equated eternal life with earthly misery. Besides, I figured, if others could do it, so could I. And why wouldn't I have thought that?

I managed to kick cigarettes, at least temporarily, but only because I used smokeless tobacco instead. It was odorless, and much easier to hide. Then one day someone saw me buying a tin of Skoal at Chuck's Café in West Grove and told the preachers. The next Sunday, as the instructional conference was winding down, Bishop Henry momentarily deserted his usual impersonal comments and confronted me.

"Ira," he said in a firm tone. I jolted, fully alert. I'd never been addressed by name in any previous instruction class. Panicked thoughts flashed through my mind. This could not possibly be a good thing.

He continued. "An English neighbor stopped in and told me that he saw you buying tobacco at Chuck's Café. I, of course, hoped it was not true. But I wanted to ask you here."

Sadness, or what he figured passed for it, lined his face. He looked right at me. The other preachers sat there, mostly looking at the floor.

"Is it true?" Bishop Henry asked simply, still gazing at me intently.

I sat there, almost frozen with shock and surprise. Fear and desperation rippled through me in waves. Hot denials sprang to my lips. Who in the world could have seen and tattled? Which English neighbor would be so idiotic, so stupid, as to go to my bishop and tell him what he saw? But, after a few eternally long seconds, during which a thousand scenarios flashed through my mind, I looked right back at him. In the eyes.

"Yeah, I guess it is true," I admitted ruefully.

He arched his eyebrows and looked officially and properly grieved. Still, he smiled a sad smile.

"I'm very glad you were honest. If you had lied, it would have made things a lot worse," he said kindly. "But," he added somberly, "this will, of course, delay the date of baptism until we can see true fruits in your life."

I nodded, still stunned. And then, mercifully, Chris and I were dismissed. I stumbled from the room, my mind in turmoil.

And that's the way it went. Over the summer, I stiffened in resistance. Fretted inside, vehemently. What did they think I was, some lame-brained weakling? And by late July, I was traveling on the same path as the last time I had tried to join. With each passing week, I became more convinced that I couldn't make it. It was just too hard. I didn't want it that badly.

Then came August.

20

My brother Titus was working the home farm that summer. A tall, lanky young man of twenty-three, he was in a serious relationship with Ruth Yutzy, Marvin's older sister. The two of them had dated a few years earlier, broken up for a couple of years, and now had gotten back together. And when that happens, it usually doesn't take long—any astute observer could see that their wedding was not too far off. Probably the next spring.

On August 3, 1982, a warm, muggy summer evening, Titus hitched up his powerful stallion and headed out the drive. He was going to Ruth's place for supper. Some of the Yutzy clan was gathering for a wiener roast. I remember seeing the open buggy, hitched to the stallion, as they clattered away. He arrived at Ruth's house, and they all had a loud, jolly time, laughing and feasting on hot dogs. After supper, the boys, my friends Marvin and Rudy among them, decided to go swimming in the pond out in the field west of the house. They splashed and swam. Frolicked and laughed. Since there was no diving board, they took turns pitching one another into the air and out across the water.

Then it was Titus's turn. A boy stood on each side, cupping his hands. Titus stepped into their hands, balanced himself by placing his hands on their shoulders, and shouted, "Go!" They launched him up and out. He sliced cleanly through the air, then bent and dove straight down into the water. So clean was his dive that he created hardly a ripple on the water's surface.

The others stood about. "What a beaut!" they said. A perfect dive. Seconds passed, but Titus did not resurface. Then more time passed, and the boys grew restless. One of them, wading out from shore, suddenly bumped into Titus just below the surface. He had drifted back in. Marvin and Rudy grabbed him and pulled him onto shore, where he coughed and sputtered. He had almost drowned.

On his beautiful dive, Titus had hit the bottom headfirst, crushing his fifth vertebra.

When the news reached us at home, it was dark, and I had already gone to bed, although I was not asleep. A vehicle came barreling into our lane. Through the open window I could hear the engine roar and tires crunching on the gravel. Shadows bounced and pitched on my bedroom walls. Then the vehicle slid to a halt in our driveway. I heard a truck door slam, followed by a staccato of footsteps up the walks and a great clattering up the steps.

I was annoyed. *Doesn't whoever it is know that it's bedtime? People are trying to sleep here.* Then I heard my sister Rachel's voice, speaking a rush of words so fast I could not grasp what she was saying. "A terrible accident . . . Titus . . . dive . . . pond . . . hospital . . . bad . . . can't feel anything." Then came my dad's voice, calm and disbelieving. Then hurrying steps in the house as he and Mom prepared to leave with Dick Hutchins, the English man who had brought Rachel to our house. I got up and was quickly told what had happened. After they left, I returned to bed, but I did not sleep that night.

The next morning we learned that Titus had been flown to Iowa City in a helicopter. *A helicopter?* I thought. *It must be bad.*

Mom stayed at the hospital, but Dad returned later that day, looking drained. He tried to put on a good face, but I could tell he was shaken. The doctors' diagnosis had been grim. Titus was paralyzed. They would do what they could. Some feeling might return. But they thought not. We listened in a haze of disbelief. The words were clear, but we could not grasp them. The first full day passed in slow motion.

When the second morning dawned, we got up and did the chores, then ate a somber breakfast. No one was really hungry. As was the custom in our home, after breakfast Dad took his German Bible and read a passage out loud. We then knelt for morning prayer, which was always recited from a little black prayer book. Dad didn't use the book because he knew the prayers by heart. He got through the five-minute prayer with no trouble until the end, which closes with the Lord's Prayer. With barely a pause, he began the familiar refrain, his rich, mellow voice rising and falling in the rhythmic, comforting flow we'd heard a thousand times before: "*Unser Vater in dem Himmel, geheiligt verde Dein Name. Zu uns komme Dein Reich.*"

"Our Father Who art in heaven, Hallowed be Thy Name. Thy Kingdom come—"

Abruptly his voice broke, and he faltered. He struggled silently for some moments. Through the vast gulf that separated me from him at the time, and in the grip of my own shock and grief, my heart cried out for him. A tough, stoic, hard-bitten old Amish man. Broken. Hurting. In anguish before God. For his son. Fighting emotions he could not show.

He wept silently and cleared his throat. Began speaking again, then stopped. Silence. Struggle. Cleared his throat again. But then he said the words, and I have always believed from the bottom of my heart that he meant them with all of his: "Thy will be done on earth as it is in heaven."

The tragedy invaded every breath and corner of our lives that summer, fall, and beyond. The weeks crawled by as we absorbed the heavy truth. Titus would never walk again. After some months at the hospital, he moved to the rehab center for many more months. And then, sometime that winter, he came home. In his wheelchair.

The Amish have one of the strongest and most efficient support structures in existence. When tragedy strikes, the community rallies around and provides whatever physical and financial support is needed, as it did for us. But the system is also lacking in at least one very important aspect. It offers no real way to cope with the emotional aftereffects of tragic events, especially unexpected ones. This is not a criticism, merely an observation. It's just the way it is. Communication is sparse or nonexistent. Feelings are quashed. One is expected to accept and bear one's burdens in silence. And one does.

This stoicism comes from a mixture of faith and tradition. Underlying everything, there rests a degree of faith. The actual degree of faith depends on the individual person, of course. But on the surface, often, the structured response to tragedy is a recitation of broad generalizations, like baptismal instructions. Traditions, going way back. Traditions that will endure as long as the Amish endure.

And that's what the public sees and hears. Both the English public and the Amish public.

After the accident, I pulled back from the brink of one more rebellious explosion and continued taking instructions for baptism. We were all in shock, and it was unthinkable now for me to even consider any alternatives. There was too much to do. I was needed to stay home and take care of the farm. I wasn't that willing, really. I didn't care for farming. But there was no alternative. Anything less on my part would have been considered hugely selfish. Especially since I was already joining church. So I stayed.

And the following month, on a Sunday morning in mid-September, the day of my baptism arrived. Bishop Henry Hochstedler would officiate. That morning, in the Obrote conference, we received our final instructions and then walked back to join the congregation for the final time as nonmembers. We sat on a bench specifically for us, directly in front of the preachers' bench. Soon the preachers returned as well, and the service proceeded. After the opening sermon and Scripture reading, Bishop Henry stood and preached the standard baptismal sermon, going on for well over an hour. And as the end approached, he paused. Then he turned and addressed us. If we still felt as we had earlier that morning, we should get down on our knees.

We had reached the ultimate moment. Too late now to turn back. Not that I would have considered it, even remotely. Not now. I had forced myself to trust all those vacant promises, the cultural clichés that told me if only I joined and settled down, everything would work out. That I would never regret this choice. Of this I was assured, countless times, over and over.

It was like swimming across a raging river, fighting the silent, hungry undertow of the waters. Fighting to stay afloat. And now I had crossed more than halfway. I was approaching the distant shore. It made no sense to turn back. There was only one path open, one way to swim—forward.

We slid from our bench and knelt. Chris—the bishop's son—and I. The deacon approached, hovering off to one side, holding a small pitcher of water. The bishop stood before us and paused. All was silent. It was a holy moment. All in the congregation strained to see, to witness this event.

And then the bishop spoke. "Do you believe and affirm your belief that Jesus Christ is the Son of God?"

We repeated the refrain as we had been told to do that morning in our final class. I spoke first. Then Chris.

"Yes, I believe that Jesus Christ is the Son of God."

"Will you remain steadfast to the church, whether it leads to life or to death?"

"Yes."

And then a few more rote questions. We answered in the affirmative. "Yes."

Bishop Henry paused again. "Before we go further, these two applicants have requested our prayers. Everyone please stand." The congregation stood as we remained on our knees. The bishop intoned the short prayer from a little black prayer book, his voice rising and falling in an almost hypnotic flow.

Then the prayer was finished, and the congregation was seated. The bishop stepped up and cupped his hands over my head, and the deacon stepped forward, ready with his pitcher.

The bishop proceeded with practiced ease, the words rolling from his tongue, "Upon your confession of faith, I baptize you in the name of the Father . . ." The deacon sprinkled a few drops of water on my head. ". . . in the name of the Son . . ." Another sprinkle. ". . . and in the name of the Holy Spirit." Final sprinkle. "Amen." The bishop then flattened his cupped hands and wiped the water drops into my hair.

Then he stepped before his son. Repeated the refrain, while the deacon sprinkled water during the proper pauses. We were now baptized. The bishop turned back to me and extended his hand. "In the name of the Lord and the church, arise," he said. I grasped his hand and stood. We greeted each other with the holy kiss. He did the same to his son.

We stood there, Chris and I, full members of the Old Order Amish church. Bishop Henry officially welcomed us. We were now no longer pilgrims and strangers, he proclaimed, but brothers in Christ, in the church of God. I was twenty-one years old.

I looked at him as he spoke to us. He was smiling in genuine welcome. If fragmented memories of my rough and wicked past flashed through his mind at that moment, he didn't let on. The wild and wayward son, the wanderer, had taken the long road. But now, at long last, he was home. Safely in the fold. Safely inside the box.

I'm sure his joy was genuine and sincere. As it was for my parents. Dad would never have told me, but he was relieved and truly happy that I had actually joined the church. And Mom's joy shone from her face as she smiled and smiled. I had put them through so much. But they gladly forgot the past, gladly forgave all I had done, and simply rejoiced in this moment.

I had done it. Gone all the way this time. But even as I stood and joined my brethren after the service, even then, a strange emptiness lingered inside me.

There had been no epiphany, no sudden explosion of light and awareness. Or joy. Actually, other than the stress of the ceremony, there wasn't a whole lot of anything, except a nagging feeling that somehow I had just walked through a doorway into another place, a place from which it would be impossible to return.

I felt pretty much the same as I always had these past five years. Confused. Half-scared. Trapped. Resigned. And, deep down, desperately lost.

21

AFTER TITUS'S ACCIDENT, he remained in critical condition at the Iowa City Hospital for several weeks. He had faced death back in that farm pond and had barely escaped. It was a close thing. Very close. Had the wind been blowing away from shore, the waters would have swept him out toward the center of the pond as he hovered, powerless to move, just below the surface. He would have died. As it was, the wind was blowing toward the shore and, thus, drifting him in. He had been under the water for close to two minutes.

After moving out of intensive care, he remained hospitalized for several months before being transferred to a rehab center in Waterloo, Iowa. And there he began the long, arduous process of learning how to live as a quadriplegic. Most quads are paralyzed from the neck down and don't even have the use of their arms. But a tiny bit of fortune smiled on Titus that terrible night. Although technically a quad, he could freely move his arms. Not his fingers—they were curled and lifeless. But he had his arms. And his brain.

Still reeling from the shock of this harsh new reality, we slogged on with our lives week to week. Dad and Mom spent a lot of days with Titus. Especially Mom. She stayed at his bedside for days on end, both at the hospital and later in rehab. Once or twice I stayed with him for a couple of days. We struggled as we spoke. It was beyond strange to see my brother, chopped at the core, felled like a maturing oak before its time, and forced to enter a new existence, a new world. It was one I could observe but never, never comprehend. We talked of life as it had been, from our memories. We flinched and hedged from speaking of life as it was and as it was to be. But ultimately, we did even that. Awkwardly, almost lightheartedly, because that was the mask Titus wore.

Although well meaning and certainly helpful, many of the Bloomfield Amish people turned into annoying pests. Eager, hungry they were, for all the latest tidbits. So they could send them on down the gossip pipeline, as interpreted by themselves. They launched an incessant barrage of simple questions, with one repeated a thousand times: "Does he have a lot of pain?"

What does one say to that? "Well, let me think. He's lying there with a metal frame screwed to his head. He can move his arms. And his head. Nothing else. What do you think? Would that be painful?" It got so we'd just mumble incoherently and turn away.

We had no medical insurance. Most Amish people don't. Titus was twenty-three and technically on his own, so Dad wouldn't have been responsible for the bills. He could have shrugged his shoulders, bemoaned his son's plight, and feigned helplessness.

But he took it upon himself to look after the bills. To accept them as his own. The decision created a lot of problems. The bills continued to mount, and there was no way Dad could pay them

all. He conferred with the Bloomfield church fathers. They counseled him to accept the bills. Somehow, the church would help
get them paid. The church fathers also appealed to other Amish
churches in surrounding communities. But it seemed hopeless.
The bills were mounting inexorably, tens of thousands of dollars.

And then a strange and wonderful thing happened. It came
out of Aylmer. Old Aylmer, the place where I had been born and
raised. Aylmer, still the shining city on a hill. At least publicly.

The Aylmer people were quite shocked by the news of the
accident, and they were sympathetic. In the next issue of *Family
Life*, preacher Elmo Stoll, Aylmer's powerful undisputed leader,
wrote poignantly of our plight in his lead editorial. Briefly he
wrote of Titus and of the tragedy that had struck that August
night.

Titus, he concluded, would never walk again. And then Elmo
smoothly switched into fund-raising mode, imploring those who
had read Dad's stuff for all those years, who appreciated his efforts
and his work, to send what money they could spare to help with
the mounting hospital and rehab bills. It would be a chance for
them to express appreciation to my father for his years of tireless
labor as a defender of the Amish faith.

We read Elmo's words in that issue and marveled. The man
could tug at the heartstrings, that's for sure. But would his efforts
produce any assistance for us?

We didn't have to wonder long. Within days the letters started
arriving and continued for days and weeks after that. And weeks
after that. Stacks and stacks, as many as fifty to one hundred letters
and cards in a single day. Short scrawled notes, expressing sympathy and support. Little cheerful homemade cards, sometimes
roughly colored by a child's hands. And always, a bit of money. In
some, as little as a dollar bill. Most others held more. Checks of
fifty, a hundred dollars. A few for as much as a thousand or more.

We were astounded and grateful. Traumatized by all that had just happened, we marveled at the blessings that literally poured in. And that's how the eighty thousand dollars was paid. *Eighty thousand dollars*, the total for Titus's hospital and rehab bills.

It was remarkable, the way it all worked out. An incident like that is probably almost unique to the Amish culture. Not exclusively, but almost.

● ● ●

Before the accident, Titus and Ruth Yutzy, Marvin's older sister, had been planning to get married. To settle in as a Bloomfield family. And as the reality sank in for us, it sank in for Ruth, too. The man she loved, the man she planned to marry, would never walk again. Not only that, he would require a lot of care. Every day. For the rest of his life. For her, it was a brutal time, a time of testing the true measure of her love for Titus.

Amazingly, or maybe not, Ruth never wavered. She was by his side as he was rushed to the hospital the night it happened. She stayed by his side throughout his long journey from hospital to home. And their relationship survived even those treacherous, rocky waters. I don't know what he would have done, or how he would have made it, had she left him. But she didn't.

And for Titus, too, it was almost beyond endurance, the thing he was now forced to bear. The desolate landscape in which he found himself. The rest of us were still back in the world he had just left. A world to which he desperately wanted to return.

In both our worlds, we knew he never would. We couldn't grasp it. But we knew.

Titus had always been active, always excited about life, and always busily pursuing his next grand project, his next shining city just beyond the bend. Titus was always optimistic. Always strong, always striding forward. And now all that was gone. All he had ever known. Snuffed out in an instant. He would never walk again. It's tough to get your mind around a thing like that.

The months passed, despite the fact that each day seemed like a week. Titus gradually gained enough strength to balance himself on a wheelchair. Learned to feed himself. Learned to gain as much freedom as a person in his position could attain. And then the day arrived, in late November, that he came home. We had prepared the house, widening doorways, pouring a new concrete walkway that snaked back and forth up the grade of the hill to the house.

We rolled him up on his wheelchair, wan and white and weak from the long ordeal. He smiled and smiled. He was home for the first time since that August night so long ago. We soon adapted to the reality of having him there. It affected all of us deeply.

We had a special buggy built for him. A top buggy, with a standard seat up front for the driver. But the back part was empty and bare. The rear wall of the buggy was hinged and latched so it could be dropped down and used as a ramp. We pushed Titus up in his wheelchair, lowered and attached the safety bar, and strapped his chair down. It would be a death trap in an accident, but it worked. Fortunately, there has never been an accident with the rig. Not to this day.

As for me, I worked halfheartedly on the farm. There was no one else to do it, now that Titus was unable to. Stephen had married Wilma Yutzy, Rudy's older sister, a few years before, a few months after Rachel's wedding. He and his bride moved to an eighty-acre farm a mile south of ours. Of course, his little farm blossomed. Whatever Stephen set his hand to always blossomed.

So the job of tilling the home farm fell to me, and I unwillingly took up the yoke. I had turned twenty-one on my last birthday, which is the coming-of-age year for most Amish youth. After twenty-one, the money you earn is your own. I had planned on working construction with a local carpenter crew, but now those plans were dashed. And besides, one other thing bothered me.

I had left home three times as a teenager. Had been gone for well over a year and a half, thereby depriving Dad of the labor that was rightfully his. So I offered to work for an extra year at home for no pay. No one suggested that I should. I just offered on my own. That seemed like the least I could do, the right thing, the manly thing, what with all the other stuff Dad had going on right then. Dad was surprised, befuddled even, but he accepted my offer with the understanding that during slow times on the farm, I would still do some construction work and pocket that pay myself.

And that's what I did. Labored an extra year on the farm at home for free. And to be honest, things about the farm rapidly deteriorated that year. I detested farming and everything associated with it—horses, cows, plowing, planting, milking, and all the attention to detail that is required for a successful operation. Still, I struggled on, trapped by circumstances beyond my control. Trapped as a member of the Old Order Amish church. Just trapped in general. Maybe God was punishing me for my wild and wicked past.

Meanwhile, my social life in the Bloomfield community continued. Marvin and I continued to hang out. Our close friendship had endured. We had journeyed together now for years. To distant lands and back again. And we had stuck together through it all. Not that we talked about it much. But we were quietly comfortable around each other, as old friends are.

One Sunday evening at the singing, Marvin and I loafed around, talking about nothing important, just inane chatter. Suddenly he turned somber and gulped a few times.

"Can I ask you something?" he asked, his voice flat and serious.

"Sure," I said. "What's up?"

He paused. Then, "Would you ask your sister Rhoda if she would have a date with me?"

I wasn't too surprised. Over the years, Marvin and I had hung out in each other's homes countless times. We were practically members of each other's families. I was instantly and instinctively pleased. He would make a fine brother-in-law.

"Sure," I answered. "I'll ask her this week. You want to bring her home next Sunday?"

He nodded nervously. And we switched back to normal settings. To be truthful, I didn't know how Rhoda would react. She was now a beautiful girl of eighteen. The hounds bayed close and distant. Undeterred, she had already sent more than one would-be suitor packing.

The following week, I asked her if she would date my friend. I was about as nervous as Marvin had been when he asked me to ask her for him. This could be a touchy thing. Amazingly, or maybe not, Rhoda didn't seem too surprised. After only a moment of reflection, she agreed. The following Sunday night after the singing, Marvin proudly escorted her home in his new top buggy. My best friend and my little sister.

Within months, they were going steady. I watched them with a tinge of sorrow. As their relationship grew, my friendship with Marvin took a backseat. It was still as strong as ever, but now my friend had more important things on his mind, things that demanded his immediate attention. Now both of my best friends, Marvin and Rudy, were dating. Maybe it was time for me to make a move as well. Start dating. Settle down for good.

I already knew exactly which girl I would ask.

22

NATHAN WAS THE SILENT SON. The youngest child, he never really connected with the rest of us, except on a surface level. Even when Nathan was a little boy, my father, perhaps exhausted from life's heavy and incessant demands, pretty much ignored him.

Whether or not he meant it that way, Dad didn't seem to know or much care that Nathan even existed. No one noticed, at least not to the extent that one would see it reflected in the child. But from Nathan's earliest days, Dad planted, firm and deep, the seeds for the bitter fruits of rage and confrontation once Nathan reached adulthood.

Stephen, Titus, and I had always hung together growing up. We were known as the "three little boys." Nathan, tagging along five years behind me, played and hung out with our sister Rhoda. The two of them were fast friends, and they did everything together as children.

Nathan was sociable enough and made friends in Bloomfield.

But compared with his loud, rather opinionated, older brothers, he always seemed shy and withdrawn. He turned sixteen a few months after Titus's accident. As the baby of the family, Nathan was close to his mother. He hovered over her and protected her.

Dad didn't harass him that much, not the way he had harassed me years earlier. Mostly he scolded and admonished Nathan for minor infractions now and then. Always quiet, Nathan quickly drifted further and further from his home ties, such as they were. Of us all, only Rhoda made much of an effort to understand him.

And by a few months after his seventeenth birthday, Nathan had crafted plans to leave. Somehow he contacted my old buddies in Valentine, Nebraska. They were eager for another good Amish worker from Bloomfield. And so, like me, he would set out to see for himself that other world. Only he was a bit younger than I was when I left.

But he would not do what I did. He would not sneak away at night. Maybe he still remembered Mom's shock and tears the morning of my first absence, or the evening we disappeared in the old green Dodge. Maybe he just couldn't bring himself to treat her like that. Or maybe he had other reasons altogether.

He told me one morning, a warm, balmy day in February, that he would leave after lunch. An English buddy would park out at the end of our long lane. Nathan would walk out to meet him. And leave. Just like that. In broad daylight. At seventeen. He would do that.

Despite myself, I was intrigued and ashamed. Intrigued that he would actually walk out during the day. And ashamed at my own cowardly departure years before. I had sneaked away, not done it openly, like a man.

I worked about the farm that morning, but it was tense. The hours dragged. Finally noon arrived. Mom had cooked our meal.

We sat around the table and ate in our normal state of restrained tension.

After the meal, Nathan disappeared into his bedroom. That wasn't unusual. We always took a short nap after lunch. He quietly showered and packed his things in a light duffel bag. Mom was outside puttering around, maybe hanging laundry on the line. I don't remember.

Finally Nathan emerged from his bedroom and walked up to Dad, who was sitting in the living room.

"I'm leaving," he said shortly, abruptly.

Dad looked up at him, uncomprehending. Then it slowly dawned on him what Nathan had just told him.

"What? No, you should not do that," he said, his face darkening into a serious frown.

Nathan just grunted and walked out, duffel bag in hand, and shut the door behind him. Dad rose from his chair and followed him to the door. He stood there, looking out, unsure of what to say or what to do.

And then Nathan approached Mom, working outside the washhouse. From a distance, I watched. I could not hear the words he spoke to her. Her face, at first turned up to him in a smile, suddenly collapsed in sorrow and fear. *No, no.* She mouthed the words. Spoke them. I drifted nearer.

Then Nathan turned and walked away from her. Down the gravel drive, the long half mile to the road.

He had gone only a hundred feet or so when she began to call his name, beside herself with horror. Fear. And love.

"Nathan, Nathan, come back," she cried. "Nathan! Nathan!"

He was her youngest son, her youngest child, her baby. And in that instant, my mind flashed back through the years to another place and time. Back to our childhood in Aylmer. The morning when he left for his first day of school. She had packed his little lunch box, and he walked proudly out the door with Rhoda and me. It had been hard for her to see him go, to release him, even then, her six-year-old son, in first grade. As we walked down the gravel road toward school, Mom had stood at the porch door on the west side of the house, watching. And every hundred yards or so, Nathan turned and waved at her. She waved back at him, smiling through her tears. He trudged on with us, then stopped and turned again. She was still standing at the door. He waved. And she waved back. And so on, until we walked out of sight.

And now she stood heartbroken, in a frenzy of dread and fear and grief, and watched her youngest child walk away again. Not to school, from whence he would return that afternoon. But away from her, from our home, away into a cold and fearful world she had never known. A world in which she could not protect him, care for him, or watch over him while he slept. Her little boy, her baby.

And this time he did not turn and wave.

"Nathan, Nathan," she cried, sobbing. "Don't go. Come back. Come back home. Nathan! Oh, Nathan!"

He hesitated only slightly but did not break his stride. Head low, he walked on. Not looking back.

As the distance separated them, her voice faltered, but still she called. Sobbing almost uncontrollably, she stood there. Calling and calling his name. Calling for him to return.

And that's why most Amish youth leave at night, the ones who go, with only a note under the pillow to announce their absence. Because they don't have the strength to walk that brutal road as Nathan did. Because they could not endure the mental trauma or live with the searing memories that could haunt a man for life.

In the house, Dad stormed about aimlessly, fuming. In the yard, my mother stood there, still sobbing softly, watching the receding figure of her son.

He reached the road and got into his friend's waiting car. They disappeared to the south in a cloud of dust.

I approached my mother. Stood there silently. And then, for the first and only time in my life, I held her in my arms.

"You have to let him go," I said, my voice breaking. "You have to let him go."

She tensed in my arms, trembling, looking into the distance to the south, focused entirely on what she had just lost. Then she pushed me away and walked blindly back into the house.

23

At home, we settled into postaccident life, life with the "new" Titus. Titus was extraordinarily brave. Or perhaps just resolute in the face of the new reality that was his world. And we were brave too, all of us. We stoically accepted the tragedy. I don't remember even once seeing any of us breaking down or weeping aloud. We kept everything, the shock and horror of it, firmly locked inside. Dealt with it—except we never really did. In time, a dull sense of resignation seeped through us, followed by acceptance, and we proceeded forward from that point to the present day.

The months crept by. Day followed day, and week followed week. I plodded through the motions of farming that year. Tilled the earth. Planted corn. Milked the cows by hand. Rhoda was right there, by my side. Helping where and as she could, even in the fields. And when she wasn't with me, she was inside, comforting Titus and helping Mom as best she could.

She was strong and resilient, my younger sister. Always of good cheer, even when there was little cheer to be found. But she prevailed and, over time, helped sustain us all with her inner will and her strength.

From what we heard, Nathan was surviving well, working hard in the vast wastelands of the sand hills of Valentine. His experience was quite different, though, from mine. I was part of a group of buddies. He was alone. And that, I think, is one reason that he returned within a few months of leaving. He would lurk about silently at home for about a year before finally leaving for good.

Having tasted the outside world more than once now, I instinctively held on to what remnants I could of that world, most notably making and maintaining friendships with surrounding English people. And Chuck's Café in West Grove was the natural site for that, the best place to establish real contacts with the local English.

Chuck and Margaret Leonard ran the café and service garage. It was a ramshackle little place, but comfortable and welcoming. Margaret, or Mrs. C as we called her, assisted by her married daughter Linda, bustled about in the kitchen, cooking meals for all the hungry locals. A caring woman, Mrs. C always asked how Titus was doing and clucked in sympathy. Chuck, clad in old, grease-stained, dark green coveralls, fussed and swore in his little shop, words flowing from him in a disjointed stream as he labored at repairing tractors and trucks for the local farmers.

I was hungry for an outside connection, and this simple, solid, southern-Iowa family never blinked but, rather, accepted me as one of their own. I was welcomed into their home as well. I stopped by many times to watch a bit of Saturday afternoon football. Or after hours, just to chat and gossip. I even developed a friendship with Father Mark, their priest, who enjoyed hanging out at the café in his spare time, relaxing with the common folk.

Every chance I got, I rode up with Fry, our old riding horse, tied her to a telephone pole in the churchyard across the road on the corner, then sauntered into the café through the rickety, spring-loaded screen door that closed behind me with a flat, thwacking sound. I usually knew who would be there from the vehicles parked out front. I reveled in the boisterous greetings, the comfortable pleasantness of the place, the chatter, the ribald jokes, and the rowdy conversations. And we just hung out, drinking coffee and swapping tales of this and that—sometimes based in truth, sometimes not.

To me, the little café was a safe haven in a surreal and uneasy world. I deeply treasured every minute of my time there. Dad instinctively resisted the fact that I hung out at the café. He sternly and frequently admonished and warned me about the world that I could never quite let go. But I paid him no mind. And eventually, the fact that I hung out at Chuck's became just a fact of life. Not accepted, necessarily. But something that was unique to me and could not be changed.

At that time, there was another fact of life we took for granted. A tradition that Dad had planted in our family. I don't know if the same thing was done at his home when he was growing up. Maybe so. But after each of the boys in our family reached adulthood and joined the church, he was presented with a brand-new top buggy and a horse of his own to do with what he would. He could choose the buggy builder and pick his horse, and Dad paid for it all.

Not every youth in Bloomfield got a brand-new buggy from his father, although many did. It was something we took for granted, the Waglers of Bloomfield. Something we did not and could not appreciate for what it was. I can't remember hearing even one of my brothers thanking Dad for that gift. I know I didn't. It never even crossed my mind. He owed it to me, I thought, and I would take what was mine. Maybe it was just a sign of the lack of communication among us. It would have been the right thing to do, to thank him—the honorable thing. I'm sure we would have done it had we known that. But we didn't.

At any rate, after joining the Bloomfield Amish church, it was time for me to order my new buggy. To his credit, Dad held off on that purchase until after I'd actually joined the church. And because of my numerous adventures, my numerous flights from home, I was much older when I got my buggy than any of my brothers were when they got theirs.

At the time, Bloomfield had one buggy builder, Menno Kuhns. He was originally from Nappanee, Indiana. (That fact always reminded me of the little fat boy I had so mistreated way back when, in Aylmer.) In Bloomfield, Menno farmed and worked part time in his buggy shop. He had built my brother Steve's buggy and many others in the area. He was a craftsman, and his products were sturdy and well built. But I thought his buggies were too wide and looked a little odd. Besides, his production was sporadic at best. If you ordered a buggy from him, it might be completed in four weeks. Or ten. You could fuss all you wanted. Menno smiled kindly and continued moving at a snail's pace as he found the time. He'd get it done when he got it done, which was unacceptable to me.

So I chose another builder, one with a stellar reputation. Mullet's Buggy Shop in Milton, twenty miles or so to the south. The Milton Amish church at that time was much larger than the Bloomfield church. They'd been there longer and the community boasted more established businesses. But Milton was separated from us. More conservative. Much more hard-core Amish. They wouldn't even fellowship with the Bloomfielders. We were way too modern. Way too worldly. So they would not drink the wine or eat the bread of Communion with us. But they sure would do business with us. Money talks, I guess, in ways the bread and wine cannot.

We despised the Miltonites. Scorned them as a group. Especially their youth. Milton Jacks, we called them. They were novices, hicks, many of them, who desperately cultivated a "wild" reputation. We looked at them with tired eyes, my buddies and me. If you have to prove you are wild, then by definition you really aren't. That's how we saw it. Let your deeds, not your words, do your talking, and your boasting. No Milton Jack had ever accomplished the feats we had pulled off.

We considered them caricatures, our Milton peers. Phonies. Fakes. Kids obsessed with image, utterly devoid of substance. Their actions more often than not sank into idiotic farce. We heard the stories of how they acted. Drink a few sips of beer, then start smashing things. Mouthing off, threatening people. Because in their weird world, that's how wild Amish kids were supposed to act. So that's what they did. They were destructive and uncouth. We never had much to do with them. Even so, we were always deliberately polite when we met up with them. But we never bragged. And to the Milton youth, we were legends.

• • •

Dad and I headed over to Mullet's Buggy Shop one day with an English driver. Mr. Mullet, the proprietor, greeted us with a shopworn air. Friendly but curt. He was a slightly rotund man with a mere wisp of a beard, and a worn leather apron tied around his waist. I figured he probably couldn't grow a bigger beard or he would have, being from Milton and all. I told him what I wanted—the buggy style and interior finish—and he warmed up a bit. As he should have. I was ordering a brand-new buggy. I forget the exact cost, but it was at least several thousand dollars. Quite a sale for Mr. Mullet, and quite an investment for my dad.

Amish and buggies go hand in hand, like cookies and milk. Buggies *are* Amish. Distinctive, certainly, from community to community. At least, to the discerning eye. Yet regardless of style, buggies are globally recognizable as pertaining to one particular group. The Amish.

But that symbol is not the same vehicle it was way back when nearly everyone still used them a hundred years ago. Not when you strip it down to its structural essence. The Amish have greatly improved and engineered the simple carriage over the last few decades. Solid framing, more safety features, better lights. It's really quite amazing. Such a simple vehicle on the surface, hiding so much technology.

Amish youth usually drive a single seater. One seat, plus a shelf at shoulder height behind you, and that's it. The buggy is wired for lights and has a small dash for the light switches. Most are lined with faux velvet of various bright hues.

Mr. Mullet took our order. A standard youth top buggy, in the style common in Bloomfield. Wired for lights. My brother Stephen would install those, after I got the buggy home. For the interior, I chose black velvet fastened with silver tacks. Still clinging to a vestige of my outlaw past, I instinctively went with black. Like Johnny Cash. The Man in Black, whom I deeply admired.

The buggy, Mr. Mullet allowed, would be ready in about six weeks. Dad wrote the check for the down payment and handed it to him. He thanked us, and we left. I was excited.

In the meantime, I was using the top buggy Titus drove before his accident. Also a Mullet model, Titus had received it a few years before. And I appropriated his horse, the stallion he drove on the night of the accident. Titus knew horses, had an eye for them. The stallion, or the Stud, as we called him, was a fine specimen. Deep chocolate brown, almost black, with a flowing mane of coarse, coal black hair. Energetic, muscled, nostrils flaring, the horse could flat out move. I won more than a few road races on the way home from the singings on Sunday nights. The Stud was one of the few horses I ever loved. And the last.

24

Life in the community plugged along. Our world with the wheelchair-bound Titus became the norm. Gradually, slowly, he regained a bit of strength, rebuilding his wasted arm muscles. He could not endure much activity of any kind. He rested long and often. Our brother, and my good friend, now existed in this new, frightful state. He mostly held up well, at least publicly, and with us. But once in a while we could see the flash of desperation and fear in his eyes.

The weeks flowed on, and the months. Titus and Ruth continued dating. Ruth was at our house a lot, since Titus could not go to hers. At least not often, because of all the complications involved. They seemed genuinely happy when they were together.

Marvin and Rhoda were dating right along as well. Going steady. They, too, seemed happy and excited. I looked on with some envy. Felt the yearning, the deep longings stirring inside. Maybe I could find it too, what they had.

Love. Settling down. Contentment. Maybe. Maybe all that could be mine someday. I had my horse. My new buggy was on its way. Soon it would be time to make my move. Providing, of course, that no one else had snatched up the girl I wanted.

And then, right on schedule as Mr. Mullet had promised, my buggy was finished and ready to pick up. We headed over to Milton with Henry Egbert and his old truck and trailer. The buggy sat there in the shop, black and gleaming. The soft interior black velvet glistened in the light; the silver tacks sparkled. I walked around it, inspected it. Breathed deeply the pleasant smell of new canvas, fresh paint, and the velvet interior. I was very pleased with my new wheels. We loaded the buggy and strapped it down and headed home.

Now I was set. My own horse. My own brand-new buggy. All I needed now was a girl.

Even though there were two districts in Bloomfield, the youth still assembled for the singings as one group. At the time, there were probably about seventy-five youth. Roughly half were girls. Girls of every size and shape and height. Shy girls and talkative girls. Girls who were desperate and girls who allowed themselves to be pursued and courted. Lovely girls and plain girls. Bloomfield, like any Amish settlement of similar size, had the gamut of them all, including the one I was eyeing.

She was still quite young, having just turned seventeen. Too young, really, for a serious relationship, but she was a vision to behold—at least to me. Her eyes were blue, and her smile bright and genuine. Her blonde hair waved forward from under her covering, then swept back. She was smart and beautiful. Not overly talkative, but not shy either. She could hold her own in pretty much any setting.

I'd known her for years. Watched her blossom from a spindly kid into a lovely young woman. Been around her and her family.

I was comfortable among them all, except maybe when we were alone together, she and I. Which rarely if ever happened.

Her name was Sarah Miller, and she was my best friend, Marvin's, cousin.

She was definitely part of the elite group, among the prettiest girls in Bloomfield—in my opinion, anyway. Still, she was only seventeen. I fretted. She seemed so young. But if I didn't ask her out soon, some other Romeo would step in, and she'd be taken.

I had no idea whether she'd say yes if I asked her for a date. I was almost paralyzed by the fear of rejection.

I turned the thing over in my mind. Thought about it a lot. Then decided. And one Sunday I took the plunge, as Marvin had done before with me, and asked him to ask his cousin if she would have a date with me. He didn't seem too surprised and agreed to do it that week and let me know. The days passed, and before Sunday came again, Marvin got the message back to me.

She said yes.

And that scared me almost more than if she'd said no. *No* would have been a jolt to deal with; then it would have been over. But *yes* swung the door wide open to a world of complications, a world I had never before entered.

And then the day came. Church was at the other district, but I stayed home that day and cleaned and shined and polished my new buggy. I combed the Stud's long, tangled mane and brushed him down. Evening finally came, and it was time to head to the singing. I dressed in my "church" pants and my finest shirt. Then I hitched the Stud to my shiny new buggy and drove proudly into the evening.

I watched for Sarah that night as supper was served, and later as we sang. She smiled faintly a time or two, right at me, I fancied. *Oh boy*. Tonight I'd take her home. The evening dragged, the minutes passing slowly, as did supper and the inane chatter around me. Then the actual singing started, and the minutes crawled as we sang for an hour and a half until the last song came to a close and we slowly walked out single file. It was finally over.

The experienced daters, the guys who were going steady, didn't hang around long. They just politely mumbled good night to their friends, hitched up their horses, picked up their girls, and left. Marvin said so long, drove up to where the girls were waiting, and stopped. Rhoda walked out and stepped into his buggy, and off they went. No one even looked twice. They were a steady couple.

Then it was time for my debut.

Out in the barnyard, where I had tied him safely away from the other horses, the Stud snorted and pawed. It was unhandy, driving a stallion, because he was always wired, always tense and jumpy, always alert for any mares in heat. Or any mares, for that matter. He wasn't shy about announcing his presence, but bellowed lustily, his high, wild call ringing through the air. I calmed and scolded him good-naturedly as I led him under the buggy shafts and hitched him up. Then I stepped onto the buggy and headed through the darkness over to the house.

I don't know when all the loafing onlookers realized that I wasn't heading straight out the drive as I always had before. At some point, I suppose, after I guided my snorting horse up to the house and stopped. A shadow shifted from the knot of girls standing there. A girl, dressed in shawl and bonnet. She approached and stepped up, then seated herself with a smile beside me on the soft velvet cushion. I leaned over and slid the buggy door on her side shut and clucked to my horse. He lunged away, and we were gone. Behind us, the loafers stirred, heads turned, and tongues wagged in overdrive.

Ira Wagler was having a date with Sarah Miller!

It was so long ago. I'm sure we were both nervous. Of course we were. But I am a pretty laid-back guy (at least on the surface), so it really didn't go too badly. We chatted as the buggy rolled along the three or four miles to Sarah's home. Once we arrived, I guided the Stud up to the hitching rail beside the drive and tied him up, and we walked into the house.

I'm not sure how to describe an Amish date. It's somewhat similar to an English one, I suppose. Just two young people spending time together and getting to know each other. Except the Amish girl is escorted from the singing to her home, not off to town to the movies or to a restaurant.

The house was swept and clean. Quiet and dark. Sarah's parents and younger siblings had already conveniently retired for the night. She had a snack ready. We sat at the table, chatting. After maybe twenty minutes, we moved into the living room, where we sat on the couch. An Amish date, at least the first one, is broken into the bare essence of the way things were a hundred years ago. There is no music, no TV, no entertainment. Just a boy and a girl in the company of each other, with only their muted conversation to keep the minutes moving along. It can get awkward. I'm not saying that's what happened on *our* first date, but that's the way it can go, and often does.

A kerosene lamp flickered low in the kitchen. Back then, at least in Bloomfield, a date was not supposed to unfold in darkness. There must be some sort of lamp, some sort of light, somewhere. Under the lamp's dim but watchful eye, we sat there on the couch for the next two hours and talked.

The conversation lagged now and then, but I didn't panic. Neither did she. We'd known each other now for years. We talked of what was going on in the community and in our lives, and soon enough the clock struck midnight. It was time for me to go.

I wanted to ask her for another date. Some guys waited until the actual day, a few weeks later, to ask for the second date, but I didn't want to wonder, unknowing, for two weeks. I got up and got my hat, and Sarah walked me to the screen door on the porch. Just before stepping out, I asked her.

"Would you consider another date in two weeks?" I felt as if I stammered. The words seemed stuck in my throat, but amazingly, they came out okay. Steady. Confident. I stood there, almost frozen with tension. And she stood there looking up at me and smiled.

"Yes," she answered. "I think that would be all right."

I breathed a visible sigh of relief. "Thank you," I said. "Good night." And with that, I stepped out, closed the screen door, and walked out to where the Stud stood patiently at the hitching rail. I untied him, got into the buggy, and headed for home.

The roads were dead, except for a few other flashing blinker lights like mine. Other Amish suitors, heading home from their respective courting ventures. The Stud clipped right along, and we were home in about half an hour. And that was my first date with Sarah.

25

THE NEXT DAY, THE NEWS FLASHED through the community like a lightning bolt: Ira and Sarah. *Wow, isn't he robbing the cradle a bit? She's only seventeen.* And so on and on. Most of the guys, at least the single ones, were just envious, I figured.

Besides me—and presumably Sarah—no one was more thrilled about my date than my mother. Sarah's mom may have had her doubts, and probably did, but not my mom. She literally beamed and beamed the next day, and throughout that whole week. She liked Sarah a lot. But mostly, I think, she was happy for me. Happy that I had now seemed to find myself. And that I had found a woman. Once a guy my age started dating, it was only a matter of time. Historically, it had always been so, and Mom held fast to the belief that it would be no different for her son.

It carried so many implications, that first date. So much was accepted as fact and planted in people's minds, like seed. So many conclusions. It was a huge step for me. It signaled that at last there was for me a place of calmness and rest. That I would now live the rest of my life as an Amish man. Settle down quietly. All the past, all that wandering, was now as if it had never been.

Sure, people murmured to one another, "You can tell Ira has been around a bit, just from his bearing. The way he carries himself. The way he speaks." But that just added to the mystique. The wildness, that untamable streak, had now been broken. Sarah would see that it stayed that way.

I walked about that week in a bit of a daze. She had agreed to see me again, in two short weeks. Time flies on wings when you are in love.

Then, late that first week, a letter arrived addressed to me with no name or return address, but written in a polished feminine hand. I tore it open and scanned the end for a signature. It was from Sarah. *What now?* I quickly read the words.

She was very sorry. She had agreed to see me in two weeks, but she would have to postpone that date. Her father thought she was a bit young yet, so he had decreed that she could see me only once every four weeks—at least until she turned eighteen. She hoped I would understand that's just how fathers are sometimes.

I sighed, half in frustration and half in relief. A Dear John letter of sorts, but not really. She had wanted to see me sooner but was forced to put it off for a bit longer. Two weeks longer. Which was pretty long, when you think of it. But time flies on wings, and all that.

The days slowly passed, the fourth week eventually arrived, and I took her home again. And again, four weeks after that. And that's the way it went until her eighteenth birthday, which we both welcomed and celebrated. We were excited and relieved. Now, we could see each other every two weeks. Twice as often as before. And we did.

And time went on. Titus and Ruth continued their relationship, and their plans firmed up. In June 1984 they were married at Ruth's home. Bishop Henry Hochstedler officiated in a wedding ceremony unlike any seen before or since in Bloomfield. A bearded Amish groom in a wheelchair, his betrothed standing by his side. It was a long day, and a tiring one for Titus. But by that evening, he was a married man.

At our home farm, north of West Grove, we had built a house for Titus and his bride, just south of Mom's huge garden, between Joseph's place and our home. It was a simple bungalow with ramps outside for wheelchair access and large decks in front and rear. Titus was very much involved with its design. It was his dream house for his new world—wider doorways, a small spare bedroom, a large pantry, and heavily insulated walls. Titus even designed bookshelves recessed into the walls of his living room to accommodate his rapidly expanding library.

It was a neat little nest of a home, perfectly suited to their needs. And after their wedding, the two of them settled in.

● ● ●

I struggled on with the farming. My efforts were halfhearted and pitiful, really. Still, I soldiered on. No labor of love for me, just doing what needed to be done—planting crops, cultivating corn, hauling manure, milking cows, and grumbling at my raggedy, unkempt horses.

But it was not altogether hopeless. Even as the farm slowly crumpled around me, it still produced. The crops grew. Hay was harvested, and the cows produced milk, which was shipped and sold.

Whether or not you are a farmer, there is something magical about tilling the earth, seeding it, and watching the fruits of your labor sprouting from the earth. Something magical about turning the river bottom with a plow and seeing the dark rich ribbons of dirt flowing endlessly from the plowshare. Doing it the way it was done a hundred years ago, with jangling teams of steaming horses leaning into the harness. Hour after hour in the elements of sun and wind and clouds, day after endless day, the sweat and toil and tiredness of it all.

And so the seeds were planted, and the days passed. The tilled earth rested there, silent. We watched for the first green shoots. And one day, as the sun beat down in the humid air, they magically appeared. Tiny corn plants, sprouting from the earth. Barely a wisp of green at first, impossibly fragile. Then suddenly shooting up like weeds. In the following days and weeks, the plants strengthened. And grew and grew.

And in the muggy heat of summer, after the sun had set, we could look out across the river bottom and behold a sea of whitish green leaves, shimmering in the shadowy light of the full moon. If we listened closely, we could hear the crackling, faint and spooky but distinct, like muffled pistol shots. The sound of cornstalks growing in the night.

I saw it, felt it, and heard it all that summer.

And through it all, two bright spots blazed in the weary labor of my world. Two things to which I tightly clung for my own sanity. Every chance I had, I hung out with my English friends in West Grove. And there was Sarah.

Almost daily, usually around midmorning or sometimes after lunch, I straddled Fry, our riding horse, and we jogged the two miles south to Chuck's Café. Frankly, that's one big reason the farming wasn't going as well as it could have. I spent too much time hanging out at the café, loafing. In a sense, every minute I spent there was a wasted minute when it came to the farm. But I didn't really care. I hungered for the social outlet the café provided.

It was a tiny, classic, country place, boasting no more than six or seven tables and a small counter with four stools. I helped myself to a cup of steaming coffee and sat there and traded lies and tall tales with the locals. In time, I developed deep friendships with some of them. It was a world I treasured, without which I would probably have lost my mind.

In retrospect, I believe the café meant so much to me because the people in that world accepted me as I was. I was Amish. Dressed in barn-door pants; a battered, old, black felt hat; and galluses. I was different, but those people didn't care. I had nothing to prove to them. They had no boxes and drew no lines to hem me in. Neither did they expect me to leave my world for theirs. They seemed to genuinely enjoy my company, and I certainly enjoyed theirs. And for those reasons, I was inexorably drawn to them, to the point where I was more comfortable around them than among my own people.

There is no question that the world at Chuck's greatly hindered me from fully immersing myself back into the Amish world. My English friends were free. Free to make choices as they saw fit. Free to live, really live. Free to drive cars and battered four-wheel-drive pickups. They farmed with tractors, not with sweaty horses. They spoke of the movies they watched, the things they did that I could not do. I listened hungrily, and enviously, to their talk.

Dad must have sensed my mental state, because he did his best to keep me from that world. He hated the café because it was pulling his son from his world into a dimension he could not control. From the first, he instinctively sensed the danger. And, in time, he grew increasingly alarmed at my obstinacy. He frowned darkly when I left to hang out. He tried to warn me. He scolded and lectured me to stay away.

And then, of course, I saw Sarah. After she joined the church, we started going steady, seeing each other every Sunday night.

Our relationship was the same as thousands of others before us in the Amish world, progressing naturally to the ultimate culmination—marriage. I was always excited and eager to see her. She was beautiful, bright, and well read. She spoke articulately and wrote well. And as our relationship progressed, she fell in love with me. And she told me so and gave her heart to me.

And I fell in love with her, too. Enough so that I promised her my heart and my life. But strangely, at the very point where I should have been excited—anticipating our future together— some spark inside me rose in resistance and held me back. The doubts were small at first—the fear of committing to something as serious as marriage. And revulsion at the thought of becoming an Amish man, married, bearded, confined, and grim.

In spite of my love for Sarah, the doubts and fears multiplied and took root. Sprouted in my head like the corn sprouting on our river bottom. And as the weeks and months passed, they slowly expanded into full-fledged plants, crackling, crackling, and growing in the night.

And I subconsciously began to resist the path that should have been so clear for me. Unfortunately, resistance was followed by distancing, then by withdrawal.

As Sarah and I proceeded to each new level, I felt the pressure knotted deeper in my chest. The box closing in. Tighter. And darker. I could not express to Sarah the doubts that rose like monsters in my mind. So I closed off emotionally instead and withdrew from the woman I had courted, the woman whose heart I had claimed. It was a strange and terrible thing.

I was not honest enough to speak to her about it—where I was, and where I was going. She sensed it soon enough, though, my emotional distancing, and tried to communicate to me her fears, her insecurities, and the strength she so desperately needed from me. I refused, at that point, to admit to her the obvious. That she was losing me.

Though I did not realize it at the time, the clouds were quietly gathering in the distance. Coming together to form a perfect storm. At first I had no intention of ever leaving her. I could not have even comprehended such a thing in my heart. I would not have allowed my mind to go that far. I stumbled along, silent and helpless, and continued seeing Sarah, week after week. It was all so very cruel and so very, very wrong. But it was what it was, and I can only tell it like it was.

26

MARVIN AND RHODA'S WEDDING came in October, four months after Titus and Ruth were married. This time, the wedding was at our home. The service was held in our large machinery shed. Sarah and I were honored to be Nava Hocca. And that day, for me it truly was an honor—my best friend married my sister.

They bought a little trailer home and set it up on the hillside west of our house in the woods. And there they lived in contentment and quietness. A new, young Amish couple, starting up their own household, and soon their own family.

Dad, worn and tired, decided to divest from farming and spend more time writing. He offered to rent the farm to Marvin and me as partners. I was excited. If I was ever going to farm, it would be with my best friend. Maybe we could make it work, the two of us together.

And so Dad held a public auction to sell his stuff. Marvin and I were given full rein to purchase what we needed, all on credit. And boy, did we ever load up that day. We bought cows, machinery, horses, and equipment. Not everything Dad owned. Much was purchased by the public, outside buyers. But we bought what we thought we needed.

In his own unpolished way, Dad did want what was best for his children. Wanted to help us as he could. And he did, as he could. Gave generously, to a fault almost. But he would help only his children who remained within the boundaries of the Amish way and lifestyle. His assistance was entirely conditional upon the decisions his children made.

And so Marvin and I took over the operations on my home farm. The Wagler-Yutzy Farm, we called it. It sounded so professional, and it seemed as if it would work out. We labored long and hard in the fields. All was going as it should have, as the Amish formula of life foretold. It was also a time unlike any in my family's history, before or since.

For my parents, it was the beginning of a golden age that would last for more than a decade. They were surrounded by their married children. Six of them. Titus and Ruth lived a few hundred yards down the lane. Halfway out to the road, my brother Joseph and his wife, Iva, had settled with their family. My sister Naomi and her husband, Alvin Yutzy, and their family lived a half mile south. Stephen and his wife, Wilma, and their family set up house a mile south. Rachel and her husband, Lester Yutzy, and their family were a mile west across the fields. And Rhoda and her husband, Marvin, lived in a trailer up the hill on the home farm.

In some small sense, it was my father's empire. The Waglers were an influential force in Bloomfield, and he was the undisputed anchor of that force—the aging patriarch surrounded by his offspring, approaching the sunset of his years. There was no way he could have known that all too soon it would all be gone. Had he known, I suspect he would have treasured and appreciated those days far more than he did. Or maybe not.

My mother, too, could not have imagined what the future held in store. And just as well she did not and could not know. Surrounded and honored by her children and grandchildren, she glowed when her daughters came home to spend the day with her, sewing and canning and quilting, doing the things Amish mothers and daughters do. Those times, I believe, were among the happiest of her life.

The stage was set, or so it seemed. Set for the act in which I would soon play an important role. Where I would show that one could settle down after tasting of the world to the extent that I had. I was dating a lovely girl that I would one day marry. I was set up on the home farm with my best friend and brother-in-law. All that remained, all I had to do, was walk forward through that open door. Accept the path prepared for me. And live the life so many around me wanted me to live. In quietness and confidence and contentment, and all that.

And it went okay around the farm, at least at first. Marvin and I were busy setting up our little operation. We planned to farm as our fathers had before us. We milked a dozen or more cows by hand and kept a few sows to raise and sell market hogs. We planted crops on the rich, black river bottom and harvested hay from the northern hills. Our grain bins and barn lofts were filled to the brim with the fruits of our labor.

And every Sunday night after the singing, I took Sarah home. We were a steady couple now. One of those things that just was. But I felt the pressure of the next step closing in. After dating "steady" for a certain period of time, a couple is expected to proceed to the next level.

And one Sunday night, because I sensed the time was overdue for what was expected of me, I decided to do the right thing and ask the question.

I was nervous when we arrived at her house. I mean, who

wouldn't be? Our talk of little things ebbed and flowed. And there was a time of silence. I held her there, in my arms, looked outside into the night, and then down again into her face.

"Sarah," I whispered. She tensed and looked up at me intently.

"Yes?" she whispered back.

I fumbled for the words that were not in my heart. Words I knew I needed to say sooner or later. And it was already later. So I spoke what was expected, what she wanted me to say, what my entire cultural world craned to hear.

"Will you marry me?" I asked.

She smiled; her face glowed. She tightened her arms around me. Her blue eyes sparkled. Shone with joy.

"Yes," she whispered. "Yes, yes, yes. Oh, Ira. Yes."

I held her, looked down into her face. Her eyes were closed. She was at rest in the arms of the man she loved, the man she trusted. She was betrothed. Safe. Protected.

Except, of course, she was not. I was not the man she thought I was. I was not safe. I glanced out into the darkness through the shaded windows. There was nothing to see but the deep gloom of the night. No moon, no light, no stars. Nothing.

I was trapped inside the box, and the lid was closing. There was nothing I could do. I was lost.

That's how I felt on the night I asked Sarah to marry me.

Midnight arrived at last, and she saw me to the door and hugged me good night. I walked out to where the Stud waited patiently at the hitching rail, untied him, got into the buggy, and we rattled home through the night.

It is always a secret thing when an Amish couple get engaged. They know, and the immediate families, but that's it. There is no formal announcement. Plans are made furtively and secretively. And, of course, there are no rings. Gold and silver jewelry would reflect pride. The Amish have never worn wedding rings. The groom may give his betrothed a gift, maybe a fancy dish or some other trinket that might or might not actually be useful. I can't remember that I gave Sarah anything. I may have, and probably did. I just don't remember.

About a month before the actual wedding, at the close of a regular church service, the bishop formally announces the upcoming event. "A brother and sister have expressed their desire to get married." He names the couple and announces the wedding date, and during those few short weeks leading up to the grand event, the couple bask in the good wishes of friends and neighbors.

I had asked Sarah to marry me. And in the days that followed, we talked about a distant date. Next year, maybe next summer. That would give me some time. Time to adjust to the idea, time to prepare myself mentally. Time to force myself to go through with it, as I had done a few years before when my baptismal date loomed. I had every intention of going through with it. Maybe not right then, but soon. When the day came, I would be ready. Of that I was fully confident.

27

IT ARRIVED INNOCENTLY ENOUGH, the dark thing. One day, as I was preparing to go somewhere in my buggy, probably to church, I harnessed my faithful stallion and hitched him up. I soon realized something was seriously wrong with my horse. His head hung low, and he did not snort or paw about as usual. After we returned home later that day, I led him to his stall and wiped him down. Brought him some good hay and feed. Petted him and soothed him. He nibbled listlessly at his food.

Maybe he had a cold or something. He'd surely get better soon. In the following days I kept an eye on him, led him out each day for water and a bit of exercise. Spoke to him soothingly. But he did not improve, and as the days passed, I became increasingly alarmed. Just once, I hitched him to a light two-wheeled cart and drove him up to Chuck's Café. He seemed to have lost his sense of balance and staggered alarmingly. After we made it home, I led him back to his stall. It was time to call the vet.

But even then, I hedged. I could not and would not bring myself to make that call. Time heals, I figured. Just give the Stud some time. He'd be himself soon enough.

He wasn't, of course. The days passed. Then the weeks. His health did not improve. Instead, he became increasingly listless and lifeless. And the day arrived when he could no longer stand when I walked into his stall to feed him. He lay there, on his side, his eyes dull and glazed, his breath coming in slow, rasping gasps.

Now it *was* time to call the vet. I should have done it long before. I rode up to Chuck's Café after lunch that day. The crowd there greeted me boisterously, as usual, but I did not respond. Every person there got somber and quiet. My horse was sick, I told them. I needed to call the vet. Mrs. C waved me to her wall phone and I dialed the number. It just so happened he was in my general area, his secretary told me.

He arrived early that afternoon, a young guy from Centerville. The Stud was still on his side in his stall, unable to even get up on his feet. The vet examined him. Poked and prodded him here and there. Pried open his mouth, stared down his throat. And then the vet stood and turned to me somberly.

"He's done. Your horse is not going to get better," he told me. "There's nothing I can do. We may as well put him down."

I stared at him. I heard the words. He spoke what I had feared would come. And now I'd have to decide. I looked at the Stud, my proud horse, helpless on his side, breathing hard. It could not be. Of all the bad luck I could imagine, this was probably the worst. Something I could not have fathomed or foreseen.

I could just let my horse die on his own, I thought. *A natural passing.* But as I looked down at his proud head, now sweating with fever, I knew I could not do that. He was as good as gone. There was no sense in prolonging his agony. I turned to the vet.

"Just give me a minute," I said. He nodded, turned, and walked out of the barn.

I knelt there in the dust and straw beside my horse, cradled his fevered head in my arms, and stroked his long, coarse black hair for the last time. I spoke no words, just knelt there in silence and sorrow. Minutes passed. The vet waited patiently outside. I stood, then bent and stroked the Stud's forehead one more time. Then I turned and walked out.

"Do what you have to do," I said to the vet.

He walked into the barn carrying an ominous little black satchel. I crouched inside the doorway of the barn, watching. He set down his satchel and opened it, took out a large syringe fitted with a wicked-looking needle, and a plastic bottle filled with clear liquid. He stabbed the needle into the bottle and filled the syringe. Then he stepped over to my horse, wiped a spot on his neck, lifted the syringe, and plunged the long needle into the hard muscles in the Stud's neck. Slowly he depressed the plunger, and the evil liquid flowed into the Stud's veins.

In mere seconds the Stud's entire body relaxed visibly. He never even quivered. Just relaxed. Then his proud eyes closed in final sleep. It was over. My horse was dead. His body lay there, stretched in the dust and straw, limp and quiet.

I got up and walked outside.

After the vet had cleaned up and left, I hitched a team to our work cart, backed up to the barn door, uncoiled a long rope attached to the cart, and tied it to the Stud's rear hooves. I clucked to my team, and the horses snorted nervously at the smell of dead flesh behind them before lunging forward. Then off we went up the hill to the west side of the house, and down again on the other side, to a soft, shaded spot beside a tree-lined creek in the northern field.

After untying the rope from the Stud's hooves, I drove back

to the barnyard, gathered a massive hedge-wood corner post, a posthole digger, and a chain saw, and returned to the spot where the Stud's body lay.

The soil by the creek was moist and soft, and within a couple of hours, I had dug the hole. A grave for my horse. I shoveled the damp earth over him and piled it high.

Dusk was settling around me as I sank the post into the ground and tamped the dirt around it. I fired up the chain saw and cut the Stud's date of death into the post. Then I fastened his halter and his lead rope around the post. And with that, it was finished.

I stood there, a solitary figure in the lengthening shadows. The sun sank low, then disappeared. In the settling night, bats flitted and zipped about. In the southern skies, a white half moon appeared, then the first stars. From the brushy hillsides all around, whip-poor-wills whooped and called. I stood there, silent, unmoving for some time. Finally, I stirred, picked up my gear and turned toward home. I slept that night in utter exhaustion—a deep, dreamless slumber.

My horse was dead. He'd passed, after wilting into a weak and helpless shell, for no discernible reason. And was now properly buried, by my own hand. A signal event, unexpected and tragic, followed by a symbolic act. In my exhausted and traumatized mind, it seemed like a sign. There was nothing left to keep me here. Not even my horse.

• • •

Those around me sensed and felt my despair, but they seemed helpless to offer any comfort or assistance. There was no rage. No lashing out at anyone, no seething. I don't remember the exact moment that I realized I could not do it. A few months later, I suppose. Or maybe I always knew it, deep down, but could not face it honestly. Whatever the case, I fully and finally realized and admitted to myself that if I married Sarah, I would one day leave her. Period.

My final withdrawal from her was painful and protracted. Instead of confronting my options and making decisions, I continued mentally drifting away from her. She sensed she was losing me for real this time and fought hard to hold me. Still, I avoided the matter as much as possible because I didn't want to hurt her. What I didn't realize was that my actions and eventual choices would hurt her far worse than they would have, had I just told her how it was.

Looking back, there really was no reason why it couldn't have worked, at least on the surface of things. We were very compatible, she and I. She loved me honestly and deeply. She would have been intensely loyal. But in my heart, I felt nothing. No love. No feelings at all. Except a sense of pity for the pain I knew was coming. For what I would put her through.

During the years of our courtship, we got to know each other pretty well, up to a point. Beyond that, I would not allow her closer, would not allow her to explore the boundaries of my heart. Had I known then even a fraction of what I now know, the issues would have been confronted. I would have spoken, confided in someone. But there was no one—not one soul—I trusted enough to reveal what was in my heart. That's just the way it was.

And there was one other thing Sarah and I never did together. An important thing for any couple considering marriage, according to our preachers in the Amish church.

We never prayed together. Never approached God to ask for his blessing on our future. Never. We should have, I suppose. But we didn't. And the blame for that omission was mine alone. I was the man. In Amish culture, as in many others, the man is expected to lead. Physically. Emotionally. Spiritually.

I did not. Didn't have the nerve, I guess. And besides, I wasn't sure it would do any good. There were times when I wasn't even sure I believed in God at all.

I probably always believed there was a God, a sort of dark and frowning force. I just didn't believe *in* him, not to the extent that I thought he could or would make an actual difference in my life. I tried to believe, in my heart. But I couldn't, in my head. I'd heard about him all my life. But if he was everything the preachers claimed he was, he sure had a strange way of hiding himself from people like me.

And because we, Sarah and I, could not address the God we claimed to serve, because we could not as a couple even speak to him from our hearts, our relationship was doomed to fail.

Sometime late in 1985, I entered a land of looming, fearful shadows, a mental zombie zone, from which I would not emerge for several years. And gradually, I descended into a world of real depression. There was no diagnosis, because counseling was not an option. Requesting counseling, back then, would have been tantamount to admitting one was insane. Not that I would ever have thought of considering it, anyway. I wouldn't have known enough to consider it. So there was no help for me. The darkness would have to be faced alone.

Those were surreal days, in retrospect. I walked about in a fog of pain and silence, walled off from those around me. I wasn't angry. Only sad. And not particularly because of them. It was not their fault. They were who they were. And I was who I was. They could not communicate. I could not communicate. We didn't know how. We were never taught how. So we stirred about, passing each other like blind men stumbling in the night.

Had I been less intense or less honest, I might have squelched the doubts, ignored the depression, as most Amish youth somehow manage to squelch that inner drive, the inner hunger to know and live outside the box of Amish life. Some few probably never even wonder what's outside or, if so, only sporadically, lacking any real passion to find out. Some have vague perceptions that there is another world out there. Most decide to do what needs to be done, and they stick with it through sheer force of will.

But for me, that was impossible. I was trapped. The walls were closing in. Imminent disaster loomed. Those around me simply looked on in disbelief as I slowly sank before their eyes. In their defense, they offered what they could, which was little more than the broad, meaningless bromides I had heard all my life: "Can't you just decide to do what's right? Reject the 'world' and accept the Amish way? Really and truly, once and for all?"

In the troubled fog of those days, Mom sought me out one day and tearfully spoke to me of Jesus and how he could help me, if only I asked him. Her words came from her heart, and she believed them. And I did not doubt them, necessarily. But what she said was hopeless. At least to me. I had tried that a few times. Praying. Never seemed to do much good. Maybe my prayers weren't heard. I doubted that they were. I'd done a lot of bad stuff, possibly even committed the unpardonable sin. Blasphemed the Holy Spirit, that horrendous act about which Amish preachers often thundered at great length and warned against. None had ever, as far as I could remember, defined that unpardonable sin. What it meant to blaspheme the Spirit. But it probably applied to me and the things I'd done. Who could tell?

I turned from Mom in silence. She did not approach me again, not like that.

My father, too, troubled by my traumatized state, admonished me kindly, or with what passed as kindness for him. The Stud's death, he decided, was the real source of my problems. The reason I was depressed. A horse is a horse, he told me encouragingly. There were other horses out there, as good as or better than the

Stud had been. He even offered to buy me another one, any horse I chose. It was a generous, although somewhat desperate, gesture, coming from a tough old man like him.

But from him, too, I turned in gloom and silence. And he did not approach me again, not like that.

The days crept by. I still faced one major task, an ominous task, fraught with all manner of messiness—breaking up with Sarah. It loomed before me like the dark clouds of a gathering thunderstorm. Never for one instant did I consider slipping away. I would face her and tell her this hard and terrible thing. That I did not love her and that I was leaving. It was almost more than my exhausted mind could absorb, but I never considered any other option. The days of leaving with only a note to explain my absence were over. I would never do that again. Not to my parents. Not to anyone. Ever.

I would face Sarah and tell her. But when? How? There was never a good time for a tough job like this, but if it had to be done, I might as well get it over with.

With the Stud gone, I drove Kenny, a sad old plug of a horse, to church and the singing. Kenny was almost a caricature compared with the Stud. Big headed. Bony. Klutzy. No one in my position would normally be caught—under any circumstances—driving a horse like that, but I couldn't have cared less. Little pride remained in me for the trappings of Amish youth. And Kenny did get me to where I was going, albeit at his own snail's pace.

I don't remember where the singing was that Sunday night. After the singing, I hitched up Kenny, and we lurched slowly up to where the girls waited for their rides. Sarah flitted from the group and stepped up into my buggy. As I had done dozens of times in the past two years, I leaned over, slid the buggy door shut, clucked, and slapped the reins. Kenny plodded out the drive and lumbered down the road as the other buggies whizzed past us. We had three or four miles to go to get to Sarah's house.

I remember nothing of our conversation. She chatted about this and that. I mostly grunted in response. We traveled down the highway, then off to the side road leading to her house, the gravel crunching under the buggy wheels. I guided Kenny up to the hitching rail. Sarah moved to get out, but I held her back. Tonight I would not be tying my horse to the hitching rail. Tonight I would not enter her home.

She looked at me with startled eyes through the darkness. And I spoke to her in curt, choppy sentences. I can't remember my words to her in that moment—all I know is that I spoke to her, brutally and honestly. And after fifteen minutes or so, she walked alone into her home, stunned, crying, and heartbroken.

There is no human penance anywhere that can ever atone for the wrong I did to her that night.

• • •

The news flashed through Bloomfield. Ira had broken up with Sarah. "Oh," people gasped. "Weren't they about ready to get married?" "What went wrong? Could it be that he just can't get settled down? Can't shake the 'world' from his mind?" And their gossip, as often as not, pretty much nailed it right on.

I stopped attending the singings and instead stayed home, reading and brooding. During the week I still hung out at Chuck's Café. It was my only connection to sanity, at least the way I saw it. My friends there realized I was going through some hard times, but they didn't pry. They just quietly offered what support they could. And I held on to that world because it was a rock for me in the midst of those terrible days.

My friends and family were around me like sad shadows—

separated, silent, but there. To his credit, Marvin never confronted me in anger. Maybe he should have. But he didn't. It wouldn't have made any difference. He expressed only sadness, and we spoke about the matter only once. He broke down briefly, wept openly, a thing I had never before witnessed. And then he let it go. We were friends from way back. He recognized and respected that. And he showed me the meaning of true friendship during those bleak days.

I saw Sarah now and again, but I never talked to her much, other than an awkward greeting. She came around periodically to Titus and Ruth's house, just down the lane. And one afternoon, after spending some time there, she walked up to our home to see Mom—at least that was the official reason. But she really wanted to see me. She had some things to tell me. I walked out with her to the banks of our pond, and we sat there on the grass.

She asked about my plans, and I told her I was leaving soon. She nodded. Absently, she picked blades of grass and dandelion stems from the bank, wove them together, then looped the woven band and tied the ends together, kind of like a little bouquet. Or a heart.

"I hope you find what you're looking for," she said, looking right at me. Her blue eyes were pools of infinite sadness.

I could not meet those eyes. I looked down and mumbled incoherently. She still faced me.

"These are my people, here in this community," she said. She wasn't pleading. Just telling me. She continued. "They are my family. I could never leave them."

I looked at her, startled. I had never asked her to leave with me. I hadn't even remotely considered it. But it was important to her to tell me she wouldn't go, even if I asked. I wanted to respect that.

"I don't think you should leave," I answered gently. "If this is where you belong, stay here among your people. It's not where I belong. I just can't do it, Sarah. I'm so very sorry, but I just can't do it. I tried. Believe me, I tried. I can't do it. I'm so sorry."

It was a hard moment for both of us. I sensed the raw depths of her pain and felt the loss in her heart. But my own heart was far from her, and cold. Tears welled in her eyes. She nodded and looked away. I looked out across the pond.

We sat there silently through the eternity of the next few moments. There was nothing more to say. She stirred.

"I have to go now," she said. I nodded and rose to my feet. As she got up to leave, she tossed aside the little ring of grass and dandelion stems. After she walked away, I picked it up and held it in my hands. It was a work of art, beautifully woven, about the size of a wristband. Too beautiful to discard. I carried it with me into the house and placed it carefully between the pages of a heavy book so it would compress and dry.

Through the years, and all that flowed from them, I somehow managed to preserve that woven ring as a remembrance of the beautiful young girl whose heart I so ruthlessly crushed, whose innocence was so cruelly shattered through no fault of her own. A token of guilt and penance for me, perhaps. But also a token of that time, those harsh and heavy days so long ago, when the world first trembled, then violently shook, then slowly collapsed in ruins around two young Amish people in Bloomfield, Iowa.

• • •

I left late in the spring of 1986. Behind me lay a long and bitter trail, littered with the remains of so many broken dreams, some of which were my own, but mostly those of others.

From my farming partnership with Marvin, I took one fattened steer and sold it at market for a thousand dollars. That and a duffel bag of meager belongings were all I took from almost two years of hard and steady labor on the farm. I didn't ask for anything more. I was breaking the deal we had made, and he would have a tough go of it as it was. Now he alone would do the work we both did before.

Our good-byes were sad and short. Abrupt, even. There was nothing much to say to Marvin, to Rhoda, to Titus and Ruth, or to my parents. An English friend picked me up at the farm and dropped me off at the station in Bloomfield, and I boarded the bus around noon that day. I sat hunched on the seat, motionless, as it pulled out and headed southeast to my connection in St. Louis, then on to Indianapolis. Then south to Daviess County, the land of my father's blood.

28

I DOZED FITFULLY, slumped on the reclining vinyl bus seat. It was a comfortable seat for an hour or two—maybe even three—but not for a twelve-hour journey. The diesel choked and growled behind me as the bus rumbled through the night, on and on, hour after hour. Long after midnight we finally pulled into the station. I grabbed my bag and stumbled down the steps, bleary eyed, and scanned my surroundings for my cousin Eli. He had agreed to meet me at the station, even at this unearthly hour.

Soon enough he showed up, accompanied by a troupe of rowdy-looking friends. A band of intimidating, raucous toughs, they whooped and hollered as they approached. It was a Friday night, and they were feeling good. I gaped, mildly startled. I had imagined that Eli would come alone to pick me up so we could talk, the way we always did. But I greeted them all, shook their hands, and smiled, as if pleased to meet them. Of course, two minutes later, their names were as lost to me as if they were never spoken.

Eli and I embraced each other, smiling and greeting each other familiarly. He was my old friend from way back, though we hadn't hung out much since the troubled days of the old green Dodge. Since then, Eli had left the Amish and moved from Missouri to Daviess.

We chattered for a few minutes in our native Pennsylvania Dutch, and then I picked up my bags, and we walked out of the station. After packing my stuff in the trunk, all five or six of us piled into Eli's old T-Bird, which crouched low, sagging under the heavy load.

Eli had lived in Daviess County for a couple of years, working construction. Rumor had it that he ran with a tough, wild crowd. He lived with his older brother in a little three-bedroom single-wide in the country, a few miles southwest of Montgomery, Indiana. Redneck city, but perfect for two brothers, complete with a spare bedroom for an old friend.

Soon enough, after dropping off Eli's friends, we were there. Exhausted, I stumbled in, lugging my duffel bag. Eli showed me to my room, a tiny cubicle with four thin walls and a door, but as far as I was concerned it was a palace. More than sufficient. Luxurious even. I collapsed onto the bed, conked out in minutes, and slept solidly through the night.

The next day I awoke to a new life in a new land.

• • •

Daviess County. The land of my father's blood. And my mother's. The land that harbored in its soil the hidden saga of my family's history. The land of my ancestors, where several generations had lived and grown and toiled and died. The importance of this didn't really hit me on that first day. I was more focused on adapting to my new surroundings. My earthly belongings consisted of a duffel bag filled with mostly Amish clothes, and a little cash. That was it. I was twenty-four and pretty much broke. But that was the least of my problems.

Emotionally, I was exhausted. And tense and jittery from the stress of recent events. Not that I talked about it much, what had happened back there in Bloomfield. I mumbled a few brief details to Eli to fill him in. He'd heard some rumors floating out there on the family grapevine, but he claimed he never paid them much mind. Eli was too busy to worry much about me. And as it turned out, the stories that had traveled through Bloomfield's gossip lines were actually true. Eli *was* running wild. Partying hard with a rough crowd.

I didn't think much of it, one way or another. Eli was an adult. He could take care of himself. I had enough to deal with.

Those first days in Daviess were surreal and strange. I had left home three times before, but my last flight from Bloomfield was different. Always before, I had known in the back of my mind— even as I was leaving—that I would one day return, that somewhere down the road I would come back to the quiet pastoral life into which I had been born. Back to my birthright and the way of my fathers. To settle down, to be satisfied and content.

Not this time. This time, the future was blank. There was no returning to Bloomfield. Not after burning so many bridges. After breaking so many solemn promises—to the church at baptism, and later to Sarah. This time, it was so much more serious. I had left as a member of the church. And in the code of Amish discipline, there would be only one reaction to my choices and my bold and wicked deeds.

Excommunication.

They would cast me out. Consign my soul to Satan and all his works.

There are a lot of ex-Amish out there who claim it's no big deal to be excommunicated. That excommunication is so legalistic. So, well, quaint. And vicious. And biblically excommunication bears no weight. At least that's what they claim. But I can guarantee that even if they don't admit it, it does bother them, at least to some degree. Even though the process seems so infantile, so futile.

It is a terrible thing to be formally rejected by the only people, the only culture, you have ever known. Rejected as a heathen. Lower even than the common English. The English didn't know better, so they could not be judged, at least not absolutely. But the excommunicated do know better and thus are responsible for their sins, their choices, and their actions. And because of their knowledge and actions, they are formally cast out and proclaimed tools of the devil, henceforth to be ostracized.

All this would happen to me soon enough. The full treatment. I would be formally excommunicated, that much was assured. They'd send out a warning letter, maybe two, urging me to return and make peace with God and the Amish church before it was too late. If I ignored the letters, there would be serious consequences. It would come down the way it always did. One Sunday after church, all members would be instructed to remain seated, and Bishop Henry would proceed with the process of casting me out.

It's not that I wanted it to happen, the excommunication. But I knew it was inevitable. Things were messy. There was nothing I could do, not that I could see, anyway. And so I pushed back the thought and ignored it, focusing on the other pressing issues that demanded my energy—like surviving.

I don't remember when the first letter arrived from home, probably within a few weeks. It was from Mom. She wrote chattily of the news, the weather, her garden, and how all the children came home the other night for supper. They missed me, she wrote. Her sadness seeped from every line. I was heavy in their thoughts and, although not stated, in their hearts. I knew they were reeling from my departure, but I told myself they would work through it in time. They always had before.

I had some sense of how deeply I had hurt them. I thought of it sometimes at night, when sleep would not come. I thought of my family and of all the broken promises I'd made to them, to the church, and not least, to Sarah.

I thought of her sometimes. Mostly fragmented slivers of guilt, slicing through the shadows of my mind. But I had no regrets, other than about the way it all came down—the way I'd done things. That was bad. The heavy choking guilt closed in sometimes, but despite it all, nothing could have induced me to return. Not to Bloomfield, and not to Sarah.

• • •

Eli introduced me to his "adoptive" family, the people who provided some stability in his life at that time. They were my distant cousins, and they were Waglers. Ours was a very common surname in Daviess, which probably has more Waglers than any other locale in the world. These Waglers, this family, consisted of five brothers and three sisters, all living with their mother in one vast, sprawling house. Their father had passed away a year or so before from cancer. They were polite and genuinely friendly, and they welcomed me into the bustle and clatter of their lives.

These Waglers were big-time farmers. They owned a local grain-bin business and raised meat turkeys by the tens of thousands. The five brothers bustled about, each performing assigned duties like well-oiled machines.

I was invited to drop around every Sunday for lunch. They accepted me as I was. They sensed my troubled mind but never pried. I suspect Eli had filled them in on my less-than-honorable flight from Bloomfield and the mess I had left behind, but they never let on.

They were personable and fun to be around. They were Mennonites from Amish stock, but they'd never been Amish. And they were Christians. They attended church every Sunday and prayer meetings most Wednesday nights. They always invited me to go along. Sometimes I went, to be polite. After all, they fed me on Sundays. The least I could do was attend church with them once in a while. And church was all right, because no one bothered me with awkward or embarrassing questions.

I watched them, this clamoring, joyous family. They had recently lost their father, and yet they seemed so exuberantly alive. I wondered if they were all deceived, thinking they could possibly be Christians, living like that. So worldly—driving cars and dressing in English clothes. Sure, they talked the talk. Anyone could do that. But was it real, what they had? Deep down, I doubted it.

They were very relaxed, talked openly about their faith, prayed before meals as if talking to a friend, and laughed a lot. But they were born Mennonite. They didn't know any better. So maybe *they* could be Christians even though they weren't Amish. I couldn't. For me, it wouldn't work. The only way I could ever make it to heaven was through the Amish church. That's what I had been taught all my life, and that's what I believed.

I hung out with the Wagler clan, and the days flowed on. Bloomfield and all the trauma that had transpired there still bubbled inside me, always there in my head. I needed to be busy, so I immersed myself in work and then partied hard on weekends to fend off the guilt and the incessant memories. It was a hard and desperate time.

Even though a lot of my uncles and aunts were living in Daviess, I never made the slightest effort to look them up, or any of my cousins. And that was my loss. I could have learned so much from them. Listened to their stories, discovered who my parents really were, and so much more. All I had to do was ask. The chance was there, and I let it slip through my hands. I didn't want to see any relatives. Not on my mother's side or on Dad's side. I wanted nothing to do with them, especially the Amish relatives. They would have heard the rumblings of what I'd done, how I'd left Bloomfield. I didn't want to face them, not in that condition. So I stayed away.

During that first month, I worked construction. It was okay. But inside, the restlessness stirred like silent demons, lurking in my mind, keeping me on edge. Daviess would not hold me long. I wanted to keep moving on, to new countries, new faces, and new lands.

The opportunity came soon enough. Dean, one of the Wagler boys, planned to leave in July for the wheat harvest out west. He invited me to go along. To me, it seemed ideal—travel, work, save up a few bucks. Dean was a laid-back guy, extremely calm, and a couple of years older than me. We got along well and would make an excellent travel team.

And so we left one fine day in early July, driving west in Dean's souped-up Oldsmobile Cutlass, our meager luggage packed in the trunk. A classic eighties car, it could flat out move. We took turns driving, west through St. Louis, then on into Kansas, where Dean knew some people. He said we would hang out there for the weekend, and I agreed, mildly dubious. It was his car and his trip, but I wasn't keen on mingling with a bunch of clean-cut Mennonite kids. I wouldn't fit in. Oh well. At least I would be a stranger to them. They would know nothing of me.

29

DEAN AND I CRUISED INTO HUTCHINSON, KANSAS, on Saturday afternoon, and when we arrived, a great fuss ensued—mostly from the girls gushing over Dean. His reputation as a dashing, eligible bachelor was widely known in his circles of the Mennonite world. Mine, not so much. Dean coolly greeted them all and introduced me. The Mennonite kids were all polite, although mildly patronizing, to this long-haired, uncouth, jeans-clad bumpkin who had suddenly materialized with one of their eastern friends. I smiled at them and lurked around the perimeter of things, listening to the keening clamor of their talk.

They were different, the Kansas kids. Certainly different from any I'd ever met, even in Daviess. They were friendly, but dead serious. I saw and heard it as I walked among them. They spoke in muted voices about cultural events—politics, mostly. And they leaned left. To me, much of their talk was gibberish, but some of it was fascinating. Earnest and solemn questions like "What do you see yourself doing in five years?" startled me. Such discussions, entirely nonexistent in my past, were new to me. I was lucky to think or plan ahead five weeks. Five years might as well have been eternity.

Then, for no particular reason that I could discern, a young man approached me. He was clean cut and wore khakis and a shiny new belt. I was standing off to the side, minding my own business, when he loudly asked me what kind of music I liked. The room fell silent as his friends paused from their conversations and strained to hear my answer. After stuttering a bit, not used to such a question, I stammered that I liked Peter Gabriel's "Sledgehammer," a popular, then-current, completely rollicking but generally senseless rock song.

Shocked silence ensued. Gasps were hastily stifled. Several lovely young Mennonite ladies paled and cast startled glances at each other, struggling to cover their dismay. You could have cut the disdain with a knife. The young man smiled patronizingly. And that was the end of the conversation, since I obviously had nothing edifying to contribute. To this day, I'm still not sure whether he was trying to trap me or embarrass me or was just having a benevolent conversation with an obvious misfit.

Then everyone recovered and smiled again. A healthy glow returned to the wan faces of the shocked young ladies. I hunched down, chastised. *Just leave me alone.* Later, I overheard the clean-cut young man comment that he would like to see Alice Walker's *The Color Purple*, a very "in" movie among Hollywood's cultural elites. His friends somberly nodded that they would like to see it too. I said nothing, but I thought to myself that I probably would not want to see that particular movie, just because it impressed them so much. And I never did.

Dean and I headed out again early Monday morning, driving northwest. Destination: Montana. I'd never been through this area of the country before. It was vast, open, and breathtaking. Dean and I took turns driving and pushed on through until we arrived.

He was an old hand at this. He'd worked the wheat harvest several times before and had all the necessary contacts. He was confident he could land me a job, even though I had no experience with motorized field equipment. Eventually, we arrived in Great Falls, Montana, and left the interstate for the dusty roads that led into the country, surrounded on all sides by tens of thousands of acres of golden, rolling wheat fields.

And then we arrived at the Rossmiller family farm, a cluster of buildings dwarfed by the open countryside. There, Ben Walters and his harvesting crew awaited us. Ben, a tall, dark-haired man with a no-nonsense gaze, and his wife, Donna, were from Magrath, Alberta. They traveled south into the States every year with a huge convoy of equipment and machines and worked their way back north toward home, harvesting wheat for grain farmers. Eventually they ended up back in Canada, where Ben and his brother farmed around ten thousand acres.

Dean and Ben greeted each other like old friends who had worked together many times through the years. Then Dean introduced me. Ben looked me up and down and seemed a trifle grim. I was the perfect picture of a wild Amish guy—twenty-four years old, with curly black hair that fell down to my shoulders. I shook Ben's hand and looked him in the eye. He launched a few curt questions: "Where are you from?" Fresh off an Amish farm in Iowa. "Have you ever driven a combine?" Nope. Never driven much of anything with an engine, except a car. But I can learn. I can ride with Dean for a day or two. I'm capable.

None of the questions were personal in nature. My problems were of no concern to him. Only one thing mattered. Could I perform the work if he hired me?

And for some reason, probably because he trusted Dean, or maybe because he desperately needed help, Ben Walters hired me on the spot. Five bucks an hour. Flat rate, no overtime pay. And room and board. I was hugely relieved.

On the wheat harvest, there is little opportunity to spend money. All you do is work, sleep, and eat, day after day. This meant my wages would sit idle and accumulate until the harvest was over.

Ben had four harvesting machines, combines, they called them. Massive hulks of fabricated steel on wheels, painted John Deere green. Each one was as big as a house, with a roomy cab mounted front and center and encased in glass so the driver's vision would be unimpaired, at least on three sides. Dean and I walked out and inspected them. I was astounded and intimidated. Maybe this time I'd bitten off more than I could chew.

"It'll take a month to learn how to drive one of these," I said.

Dean laughed. "They're simple to operate," he said. "You'll be driving by tomorrow afternoon."

We rode out the next morning in a combine. Dean was at the wheel, and I perched beside him on the armrest of the driver's seat. He shifted into gear, and the combine shuddered as the thirty-foot-wide cutting blade clacked to life below us. We moved slowly forward into the field; behind us, wheat poured into the combine's holding bin. Dean coached as he drove. "Keep your hand on the lever, here. You can feel if something's wrong, once you get the hang of it." "Keep your eyes on the cutting blade, down below, and make sure the wheat falls in smoothly." "Watch out for rocks." And so on. After lunch, he got out of the driver's seat and motioned me in. Thus began my crash course in operating heavy farm machinery.

It was a weird feeling, operating such an enormous piece of equipment. A short hydrostatic lever controlled the ten-ton machine. Push the lever forward to move forward, pull it back for reverse. And that was about it. We throbbed along that afternoon, Dean keeping a careful eye on things. I remained tense and alert, always scanning for any sign of mechanical trouble.

Dean stepped out of the combine sometime during the second day, leaving me all alone in the cab. He moved over to the job he loved, jockeying Ben's semi-tractor hitched to double trailers, hauling wheat to the elevators in Great Falls, while I trundled along timidly in the fields, driving the combine on my own. For a few days after that, Ben kept a close eye on me. When he saw that I was responsible and careful, he relaxed, and I grew more and more confident with each passing day.

In the comfort of my air-conditioned cab, I drove and drove through endless acres of waving gold. And in that private zone, alone in my cab, the recent past gradually receded from my mind until it seemed far away—another world, in another life. Physically, I was a long way from Bloomfield, and emotionally, the distance lengthened each day.

I immediately connected with Donna, Ben's wife. The year before, she had emerged from a long battle with cancer. She'd licked it, at least for the moment, although within a decade or so it would return and claim her. She was a strong and beautiful woman, exuding fortitude and courage. Perceptive and intelligent, she instantly saw through my smiling facade and sensed that I was running from something in my past, that I was lost and searching. And in time, she openly confronted me. Not as a hostile force but as someone who was genuinely interested and concerned. I remained guarded at first, but as time passed, I began to confide in her. I told her who I was. What I was. The things I'd done. And she was intrigued.

At the time, I was deeply immersed in the works of Leon Uris. During our conversations, I cautiously mentioned as much. She immediately went out and bought one of his novels and read it cover to cover in a few short days, and then we discussed our opinions of it.

Ben, too, lightened up a good deal as the weeks rolled on. He was a good and decent man, slightly dour, with a dry sense of humor. He was a businessman, a farmer, and above all else, a man who walked forward into life, tall and confident. He had been born in the Hutterite colonies in Alberta. A communal branch of the Anabaptists, this society was even more closed than the Amish. His parents had left the colonies, and Ben grew up mostly outside the confines of that isolated culture. But he knew and understood what it was to break away. Through the course of many decades, he had seen his parents grapple with the pain, the struggles, and the stress of it.

I didn't realize it at the time, but this Mennonite couple from Magrath, Alberta, were providing exactly what my hungry, traumatized mind craved and cried for at that moment. Ben provided me with work, a job that required many hours of physical effort each day. He looked me in the eyes and treated me like a man. And Donna, well, she provided intellectual challenges and a tentative place to communicate, even though at that time I had little grasp of how to do so. They were there, Ben and Donna, and to a large extent, they were safe. Safe, as in a place for me to unwind from and absorb the stress and strain of all that I had just fled back east.

The days and weeks rolled by, and August came. Day after day we rolled through the fields, from midmorning until midnight or later, when the call would come over our two-way radios to stop for the night. Then we would park our machines, get out, and wait for the pickup to fetch us and haul us back to camp, where we would fall into our beds for a few hours of exhausted, dreamless slumber before getting up the next morning to do it all over again.

Sometime in August, Dean left for his home in Daviess. He did not travel the wheat harvest because he had to, but simply because he enjoyed it. He didn't need the money. It was unfathomable to me that he could afford to travel for almost two months without any concern about his future. Wherever he went and whatever he did, he was never really alone. He had his family back in Daviess. A secure support structure, always there for him in case of emergency.

And I knew they would have been there for me, too, in an extreme emergency. But in the normal course of things, I had no one. Unlike Dean, I was alone in the world. Whatever happened, he would be okay. He would somehow make it back to his family. I would not—because there was no family to whom I could return. Not in my current state.

With Dean's departure, the fact that I was alone, at least symbolically, was even more obvious. I had people around me, of course—Ben and Donna and the crew. But except for Donna, they didn't know that much about my past. I was on a clean slate, alone, among those I had never known before. No connection whatsoever to Daviess or Bloomfield. What little Dean knew of my past stayed with him and went home with him. And in the vast Montana landscape, I felt a strange new sense of freedom in the here and now. The past was behind me. Who knew what the future held? In the moment, I simply lived.

In the spirit of this vagabond life, I decided to grow a beard and a mustache. It actually looked pretty tough, especially after I took to wrapping a bandanna around my head as a standard part of my daily attire. I could have been a mean biker, the way I looked. Definitely not someone you'd want to meet in a dark alley late at night. But it was just image, with no real substance. I wondered if all the tough guys I had ever seen felt the same way. Or even some of them. Maybe it was nothing more than a sham, dressing like that.

Late August came, and with it, my birthday. I was twenty-five years old, and I celebrated alone, quietly and reflectively. I don't remember if I even mentioned it to those around me. To me, twenty-five had always been some distant, mystical age by which I figured I would be settled into the Amish faith and lifestyle. A young Amish husband in my own newly established household, perhaps with a son or daughter, moving forward into the future, content in the quiet life. That's where I had always thought I'd be at twenty-five.

But that's not where I was. I was in the remote country of Montana, vagabonding my way through life, thousands of miles from the land of my father's people, because I could not abide there. It was a bit of a jolt to realize, at twenty-five, that life was not turning out as I'd always imagined.

After the wheat harvest was done, Ben planned to travel from Great Falls over the border into Canada. He asked if I would come along and work for him. By then, I was considered an experienced, battle-hardened hand—just the kind of guy Ben needed in Canada to harvest his own crop. With my Canadian birth certificate, I could legally cross the border and work. I agreed to go on one condition. I needed a guarantee—fifty hours a week, at five bucks per hour.

Amazingly, Ben agreed to my terms. I figured his local labor market must have been pretty bleak or he wouldn't have agreed so readily. But his risk was low. They'd never worked fewer than fifty hours a week in previous years. How could he go wrong?

And soon enough, we harvested the last acre and wrapped it up in Montana. During the next few days, we disassembled machines and loaded them on trailers for transport up north. And when we left, I got my first and only experience as a trucker. I proudly drove Ben's ten-wheel dump truck, pulling a thirty-foot combine head on a trailer. I reveled in the experience. Bearded and bandannaed, I gripped the steering wheel and shifted gears like a pro. When we reached the border, I handed over my paperwork, and they waved me through—a boring moment for a real trucker, an intense, once-in-a-lifetime moment for me.

I pulled into Ben's huge farm complex and parked out by the shop. This was my first time in Alberta, three provinces west of Ontario, the place of my birth. Ben pointed me toward a small travel trailer set up behind the shop, where I unpacked my meager belongings and got mentally set for the long days ahead.

Then a strange thing happened. Great cloud banks rolled in from the west, and it began to rain. And rain. And rain. Day after day, then week after week. Such heavy, persistent rains were a rarity for the season, and as the days passed, the soggy wheat bent heavy on the stalk and then bowed to the ground. There was nothing to be done except wait. And wait. Restless, I puttered around the shop, swept, cleaned, and asked Donna for projects she wanted done. Eventually, I was stuck. There was no work. But I didn't sweat it. Ben had guaranteed me fifty hours a week. So whether I actually worked or not, I knew I'd get paid.

It rained for a solid month. It was the first time in anyone's memory that such a thing had happened. Ben stirred about uneasily, looking at the dark, spitting skies. But there was nothing he could do.

In an effort to pass the time, I commandeered Ben's farm pickup and headed off to the town of Lethbridge, about twenty miles away. There, I hung out with the other harvesters, local guys who gladly welcomed me into their group. I loved spending time with them, absorbing the clamor of their Canadian dialect. They were good guys, all of them. One of them owned a house in town, where I ended up staying for days on end, partying, vegging, and just hanging out, waiting for the rain to stop.

After four weeks of incessant rain, the skies finally cleared.

This time, it was not a temporary halt, as had happened a few times before. The sun came out and stayed out, drying the earth and the soggy wheat. After a few days, we geared up for work, silently, almost desperately.

And then we attacked—one vast field after another. The largest one was two miles square. We cut that field and many others. Day and night for four weeks we worked. And then it was done. We had finished the Alberta harvest.

It was time for me to leave that world and head back east. Back to Daviess and the people and places I had not seen for months. Ben and I settled up. He never winced, but paid me through all those weeks of rain, plus the actual hours of labor on the harvest.

It was a nice, fat check. At least to me it was. A good chunk of money. More than I had ever owned before. With the help of my new local friends, I went shopping for a vehicle. I wanted a pickup truck. A man's wheels. We located one at a shady, small-time dealership. A Chevy, built in 1979. Blue, trimmed with a wide gray stripe on its sides, and dual exhausts. It was a classic truck with high mileage. But most important, it was priced within my budget—twenty-five hundred bucks. With what I had earned from Ben, I could buy the truck, get it licensed and insured, and still have enough left over to make it back east.

It was my first vehicle since the Cougar with the 351 Cleveland engine, back in Florida. All I had to do now was come up with a fitting name. It didn't take long. On the blue, hard-plastic bug shield mounted on the hood front, I glued reflective letters spelling the word *Drifter*. It seemed so fitting for who and where I was at that time.

In the next few days I packed up to leave and said good-bye to Ben, who offered me work the following spring.

"Come on up and help me seed my fields," he said. I felt good about the offer and promised to consider it. Then I stopped at the house to say good-bye to Donna. She wished me safe travels and invited me to return again, as a friend if not a worker. And then I left them.

30

It was late October, and the nights were chilling. From Canada I headed down to Montana and stopped for the night at the Rossmiller farm, where I had learned to drive a combine mere months before. They greeted me cheerfully and put me up for the night. The next day I headed east.

I took my time, meandering back. A week or so later, I arrived in Daviess, where I discovered my friends in a tizzy. They had not heard from me in more than a month. This was, of course, before cell phones. You couldn't just call someone whenever you wanted. I had not communicated much with Eli or the Wagler family since the summer, and not at all recently. As the days and weeks passed and no word came from me, they imagined something terrible must have happened. They were ready, they claimed, to send someone on the road to find me.

I settled into the trailer house with Eli and his brother, but not for long. I could not rest in Daviess. I itched to move and to travel. And within a week or two, I was making plans to head south to Florida for the winter.

I took what money I had, loaded the Drifter, and headed down to Pinecraft, the Sarasota Amish suburb where my brother Nathan lived. There, I rented a room and found a job as a mason's helper. I had not been back to Florida since Marvin and I lived there in 1981. Nathan and his friend Eli Yutzy lived in an apartment in the very center of Pinecraft, and we hung out almost every night, playing cards and partying.

I'm sure I appeared relaxed to those around me during those winter months. I enjoyed life and, to some degree, enjoyed living. But always, deep down, a thread of desperation pulsed inside me. I was a drifter, a rolling stone with no goals and chronically short of money. I was living day to day. I had zero long-term plans, or short-term plans for that matter. It was not a good place to be—financially, emotionally, or spiritually.

And always the old thoughts crept in and tormented me. I could not squash them, could not escape. I brooded quietly, intensely. What would happen to me if I were killed? I knew, deep down, there was no hope, none at all, that I would ever make it to heaven. I'd done so many bad things, hurt so many people. I had left the Amish church for the world after promising—on my knees when I was baptized—to be faithful. Breaking those vows was a very serious thing. There could be no hope of ever righting those wrongs. Not unless I returned and repented and rejoined the church, which was not an option.

But I could not shake the thoughts of my sins and of the afterlife. I knew I was lost and frankly admitted as much. There was no salvation for me. Not in my current state. I had escaped the box of the Amish lifestyle. That was a simple matter of making a decision and walking away. But the box that bound my mind wasn't that easy to escape. Entrenched inside my head, powerful and persistent, my fear of eternal damnation would not be denied. And I could not shake it off.

Once again—in spite of myself and in spite of the fact that it had never worked out before—thoughts of returning sprouted and grew. Frightful thoughts of returning to the fold of the Amish church. It was the strangest thing. I had returned three times before over the years, and not once had it worked. In time, I always despaired, always chafed at the confines of the culture. And yet I felt that this time might be different. This time, I could make it work.

It was tricky, the way things played out in my mind. The Amish have always taught, always preached, that once the desire to return leaves, that's when you are truly lost. Because that's when your conscience has been seared with a hot iron and you won't know right from wrong. You're a walking dead man. Preachers have polished off many a sermon with tales of such people, people bereft of hope who yearned for the desire to return and could not grasp it. Tales of woe and loss and tears of regret and eternal damnation.

And in my head, I still held on to that spark, that remnant of desire to make it work. I seized on that remnant as proof that I could make it work. Simply because there was a shred of desire. Desire based on fear to be sure, but desire nonetheless. I could return. I would return. In the future, of course. At some distant date, maybe the next summer. That was still far enough away that I could consider it without freaking out. Inside me, the restlessness stirred, as it always had. Wherever I was, I wanted to return to where I'd been before. Not the real place, but the idyllic place in my mind. The place that *could* be, if only I could get it right. And do it right.

I mulled over the issue and mentioned guardedly to my friends that I was thinking of returning once again to the Amish church.

Their reactions were pretty unified, mostly a mixture of horror, disbelief, and astonishment. My "wild" buddies were incredulous. Why would someone do such a thing? I'd just torn away from Bloomfield. How could I even think of going back into that mess? It wouldn't work. Even my Christian friends, the Wagler family, responded with polite disbelief. They were much nicer about it, but clearly skeptical nonetheless. From their perspective, why would someone ever want to return to the darkness of that cold and legalistic world?

And so, surrounded by doubters, I found myself alone again. Alone and confused. But I could not shake the idea. Why couldn't I go somewhere *else* and try it? Some other community instead of Bloomfield? That way, I wouldn't have to face all those people from the past. Especially those I had hurt so cruelly. Especially my parents. And Sarah.

I still thought of her sometimes. Mom wrote to me of her and how she was doing. In one letter Mom dramatically informed me that Sarah had had a date with someone else. Another guy. Now she was gone, Mom wrote. It was too late for me to ever get her back. Mom's message was crafted to make me feel bad, but instead, I read her words and felt nothing.

The weeks rolled by, and I finally caved to the mental pressure. I decided to at least explore the idea of going back again to the Amish church. This time, I thought I might go to northern Indiana. There was a huge Amish community there, stretching from Ligonier in the southeast to Elkhart in the northwest, more than a hundred districts, total. Maybe even a couple hundred. Either way, it was a big place and a long-established settlement. I could try it there, I figured, without causing a lot of waves. They had seen about all there was to see when it came to wild youth. Besides, the place was so big, odds were nobody would even notice me or make a fuss.

I wasn't looking forward to the effort it would take to go back: moving again, getting rid of my truck, and forcing myself back into the mold. But a more powerful force was compelling me, pushing me forward—the force of fear. Not that I talked about it much to anyone, but it was there, a fear planted deep within me. The raw fear of hell and eternal damnation was the only thing that could ever have made me consider returning to any form of Amish life.

We all long for inner peace. And I was simply following the only path I knew to try to reach it. Not that there were any guarantees. Only "hope." No assurance of anything.

I had a contact in the northern Indiana area, which is probably why the idea occurred to me at all. That contact was Phillip Wagler, one of my first cousins, who was born and raised in Aylmer. I'd known him all my life. A quiet guy a few years older than I was, he had married a local girl in the Ligonier area and settled on a farm. So I located his address and wrote him a short note. I told him what I was thinking and asked if they would consider providing a place for me to live. Of course, I'd expect to pay for my room and board, whatever they thought was fair. I hoped to find work in one of the many local factories that employed primarily Amish people.

Phillip replied almost immediately, and I knew his response before even reading it. Phillip and his wife, Fannie, would be delighted to put me up and provide room and board. He was certain I'd be able to find work in the area, and he wanted me to know that he and his wife were eager to have me.

I read the words he wrote. Absorbed them. I had taken the first step, the exploratory step. Now the offer lay there before me in black and white. The doors seemed to be opening for my return. All I had to do was walk through.

Although that was just about the last thing I wanted to do,

the invisible force of raw fear compelled me to seriously consider an option so repulsive. This was a chance to redeem myself. To return. If not to Bloomfield, then at least to the fold of the mother church. Return and make good.

It wasn't easy, considering going back. But it wasn't easy, either, to consider the alternative, an eternity in hellfire. Pretty scary stuff. This was my last chance, I figured. I was twenty-five years old. If I didn't make a decision soon, it would be too late. The desire to return would leave me. And like Cain, I would wander the earth alone. Lost. With no mark on my forehead for protection.

I thought it through for a week or two. Or three. Then, in February, through sheer force of will, I made my decision. I would return, for one last try. One last attempt to make it as an Amish person. Strangely, my decision did little to relieve my inner tension. I wrote back to Phillip. I would move up in June, which somehow seemed like a safe distance. But I knew it would come soon enough. I told my friends of my decision. And Nathan. Of the choice I had made—again. He said little, but he supported me. If that's what I wanted, then that's what I should do. They all, I think, recognized instantly and instinctively that it would not work.

I tried to put it out of my mind and focus on the time I had left on the outside. June lurked out there in the distance like a Montana mountain storm, approaching slowly, relentlessly, soon to be unleashed with savage force.

It was only a matter of time. From that point, the days passed at hyperspeed. Soon March rolled around, then April. I wanted to return to Alberta and help Ben Walters with the planting that spring, so I packed up and left Florida. Nathan wanted to settle in Daviess for a while, so I dropped him off on the way. After a few days of hanging out with the Wagler family and other friends, I headed for Alberta.

On the way, I passed close to Bloomfield, so I stopped for a few days. I don't know why, particularly. To see family, I guess. I told them of my plans to settle in northern Indiana and rejoin the Amish church there. I don't know why they would have thought it would be any different this time, but they believed me. My parents smiled with joy. I was returning to the fold. That's all that mattered. Whatever I had done in the past could be overlooked, forgiven, if only I returned.

After a day or two, the Drifter and I headed into the Dakotas and then on into Canada. Ben and Donna welcomed me. By the next day, I was driving a four-wheel-drive tractor as big as a house, pulling an eighty-foot-wide harrow across the fields. For days and weeks on end, I tilled the vast fields of southern Alberta.

All too soon, in late May, it was finished. And June approached. I fought the sinking feeling in my stomach, the dreaded thought of returning. But I held fast to the plan. There was no backing out. This was my last chance. It had to work this time. It simply *had* to. There was no other choice.

I sold the Drifter in Lethbridge to one of my friends from the previous fall. After cashing out, I said good-bye to Ben and Donna and boarded a bus for the long trip back to Daviess, where Nathan would meet me. I'd stay with him a few days; then he would take me to Ligonier, Indiana, for my final return to the Amish church. One way or another.

31

AFTER AN EXHAUSTING THREE-DAY TREK, my bus finally reached Daviess. Nathan was there, waiting for me, grinning. He was doing well. He had rented a small house in Odon, bought an old T-Bird, and made friends. He was getting established in the area.

I hung out with him until the weekend. Then, on Saturday, we loaded all my stuff into his car and drove north. Four hours—the amount of time it took to reach the new land where I would try it all over again. I was running on pure adrenaline, fighting the rising panic inside me, focusing only on this final brutal sprint.

Looking back, I don't know how I did it. Given my history, this attempt was doomed to fail. I had left the Amish four times over the years. Each time brought its own degree of serious trauma, and there was not a single time I had returned with joy. Not one. Mostly it had been homesickness and nostalgia that lured me back. Or economic stressors. And after each return I realized almost immediately that I did not want to be there.

But I was stubborn. Something of my father's blood stirred in me. Unwilling to admit defeat, still trapped inside that box in my head, I would do what needed to be done. The Amish way provided my only chance at salvation, of this I was convinced. I knew it in my heart, and no one could tell me otherwise.

I wonder now if my father would have been proud, had he known how deeply his influence and his teachings had invaded my soul. How strongly his presence and the craving for his approval and his love haunted me. Despite all I had experienced through the years, I was returning one more time.

Nathan's old T-Bird pulsed along, heading north around Indianapolis toward Ligonier. Closer and closer. Our conversation was muted and terse. Nathan could not understand what I was doing or why, but he would do what it took to get me there.

And then, way too soon, we were pulling up to the farm. Phillip and Fannie walked out to greet us, smiling in welcome. Their farm was a tidy little place with a rather ramshackle farmhouse. They were childless, so there was plenty of space in their house, and they very much looked forward to having me around.

Nathan helped me carry my bags inside and upstairs to my room, then politely declined Fannie's invitation to stay for supper. After visiting for a bit, he turned toward the door, ready to leave.

I fought back wave after wave of panic. After Nathan left, I would be stuck here on this little farm, with no way to get around. Trapped in a strange land, where I knew no one but my cousin and his wife.

I walked Nathan to his car, shook his hand, and thanked him. He got in, started the engine, and shifted into gear. The car slowly pulled out, tires crunching on the gravel lane. I watched as he turned onto the paved road and then was gone, heading back to his world in Daviess.

I turned back to the house, where Phillip and Fannie stood

smiling. I walked toward them, smiling in return, but my heart was sinking. In that desperate moment, I was as lost as I'd ever been.

• • •

The days and weeks that followed are blurred in my mind, as are some of the things that happened while I struggled to settle into this strange new place. It was Amish, but it was vastly different from Bloomfield—or Aylmer, for that matter. I had always lived in small communities of one or two districts. This settlement was massive, stretching many miles in all directions. These people had been here for many generations. Some of their habits and customs seemed strange to me. Small things, probably indiscernible to anyone from the outside. Differences in dress. The area is one of the few where galluses are optional for men in many districts. Distinctive head coverings for the women. Even the cadence of their talk seemed odd. Other than that, I can't put my finger on exactly what was different. It just was, the entire area, I mean.

I settled in uneasily, always aware of my surroundings, always aware of my status in this place. I was a stranger here, in a strange land.

The first order of business was to get myself some means of transportation. In northern Indiana, the Amish are allowed to ride bicycles. In fact, the roads are practically clogged with Amish bikers, and after trekking to a local Amish cycle shop, I joined their ranks. I chose a brand-new, bright blue twelve-speed, with collapsible baskets mounted over the rear wheels. It was the first bicycle I had ever owned. And that was my transportation, except on Sundays when I drove to church in an old buggy Phillip owned.

I knew no one. People were friendly enough, and they did

their best to visit with and include me, but it was tough. I was an older single guy, and I didn't exactly fit in anywhere, under any circumstances. That was bad enough. But then almost immediately, I walked smack into a serious roadblock as the Amish bishop in the Ligonier District, a harsh, screeching man who will remain unnamed, rose like a specter to confront me.

After my last desperate flight from Bloomfield, I had been excommunicated from the Amish church. As was the custom, immediately following services one Sunday, good Bishop Henry Hochstedler had stood before his flock, sadly proclaimed me a heathen, and formally cast me over to Satan, to be shunned as an outcast. There were tears in his eyes, I was told, as he officiated over that somber little ceremony. I was also told that Mom was "sick" that day and stayed home, so she wouldn't have to endure the pain of hearing the bishop's words. I was her son. I would always be her son, excommunicated or not.

Now, after moving to Ligonier, I planned on performing my official penance there and doing whatever it took to be reinstated and have the excommunication lifted. It wasn't that unusual, what I was planning. Those who left and were consequently excommunicated were known to rejoin somewhere else in another area, for a fresh start and all. It happened, here and there, and the preachers usually understood and did what they could to ease the journey back.

On my new bright-blue bike, I cycled over to see the bishop on his farm one fine summer afternoon. He was outside, puttering around the barn. He was a short, dark hulk of a man with a large, untrimmed, red-black beard. Not that old, really, probably in his midforties, but he seemed old to me back then. He saw me approaching and paused, almost as if he were irritated at being interrupted in his work. He grimaced with what barely passed as a smile.

I introduced myself and his "smile" disappeared. He glared at me suspiciously.

"I'm here," I stammered, "to see if I can rejoin the Amish here in your church, be taken in as a full member."

I explained how it had gone in Bloomfield, the people I had hurt when I left, and how I had been excommunicated. I really didn't want to have to go back there, to rejoin, I explained. *I would also save face rejoining here*, I thought, but that fact remained unspoken. We both knew the real reason.

The bishop did not seem receptive, or even cordial. He stared at me grimly, unsmiling and hostile. I could feel his spirit, thick as smoke. Then he spoke, his rasping voice echoing across the barnyard.

"No," he said. "You will need to return to Bloomfield and make things right there. After they take you back as a full member, you are welcome to move here and transfer your membership to my church. But not before."

I tried to reason with him. "You don't understand," I said. "I really don't want to go back there. I can't go back. There's just too much there, too much bad blood."

I may as well have choked on my words, for all it mattered. He listened to me speak, but he refused to hear. Nothing would sway him. He was every bit as dense as he appeared. Denser, even. Obtuse. And hard inside, like a rock.

"I won't lift your excommunication. I will not do it. So you can decide," he thundered. "Go back and make things right, where it happened, or don't." His dark face reddened. At least the part I could see, what with his beard and large black hat and all. He was way too stirred up. He was flat out raving mad, as in crazy. And also as in angry. Every definition of mad there was. It was no use. I would get nowhere arguing with him.

What a nut, I thought. But I said nothing. Instead, I mumbled something under my breath, turned, mounted my bike, and fled from the mad bishop of Ligonier, Indiana.

Most Amish preachers and bishops are not bad men at heart, not when you dig down deep. Most want to do what they can to help a person. Somewhere, down below that somber facade, a kind heart beats. In most of them, at least. But that particular bishop, the absolute dictator of the Amish church district in Ligonier in 1987, holds the dubious distinction of being one of the meanest, flat-out nastiest men it has been my misfortune to meet. Ever. In all my wanderings, Amish or otherwise. There was no joy in him or kindness. Only rage and vindictiveness.

I should have given up right then. Wrapped up my scant affairs, left, and returned to Daviess. And I seriously considered that option. But ultimately, I could not do it. I felt stuck. I had made too much of an effort already, come too far. What would people say? I'd been in northern Indiana only a week or so. I could almost hear the snickers. Besides, that's what the mad bishop expected, what he wanted me to do. He was sure I was a fraud and that I'd give up and go away and stop bothering him. If I did that, it would only prove him right. He'd probably even smile for real, something he likely hadn't done in years.

But I refused to give him that satisfaction. Furious, I was determined to prove him wrong.

Back at the farm, I sadly told Phillip and Fannie what the mad bishop had decreed. That I would have to humble myself. Crawl. And after being restored as a member in Bloomfield, I could return. They sat there in utter shock. In all surrounding districts, my request would have been honored. Every other bishop would have fallen all over himself to assist me on my difficult journey. The mad bishop was the lone exception in all the land. But now that he had spoken, he would be supported by the others. Church politics and all. The others would be forced to back him up in his irrational decision. There was nothing to be done except obey. Quietly, carefully, Phillip and Fannie told me these truths. I would have to do as the mad bishop had instructed: return to the source of so much pain and sadness.

It was unfathomable that I would have to walk right back into the lions' den. Bloomfield. The place swarming with so many dark memories, where they knew me inside and out, all my history. They would not make it easy. It would be a tough road. But my course was set. I would do what I had to do. I had no other choice. At least none that I could see.

The following week I boarded the train in Elkhart and settled in for the journey west. The train clacked along to my connection in Chicago, and from there, the final sprint toward Bloomfield.

As the miles flowed by, I sat, unmoving. Inside, I felt almost nothing. I could not even think of what awaited me. What I would experience back in the community I had fled a year ago. I could focus only on doing what needed to be done and on getting back to Indiana in one piece.

An English driver met me at the train station in Ottumwa. I boarded the van, and we were off.

Home still looked the same. Everyone greeted me eagerly. Marvin and Rhoda. Titus and Ruth. Mom and Dad. They all seemed happy to see me, especially now that I had returned to rejoin the church. That's all that was important, even though everyone knew I would not stay in Bloomfield. That was fine with them. As long as I remained Amish, it did not matter where.

The week passed slowly. On Sunday, Bishop Henry and the preachers would await me. In their defense, I know they were all genuinely happy that I had decided to return and right past wrongs, to come home and face the music. The Amish always welcome returning sinners. Always. It doesn't matter what they've done. Erring members who left in disgrace, those who have been excommunicated and shunned, they are always welcome to return to the fold. Of course, if they return, certain requirements are made. Repentance must be shown. Abject submission is absolutely required.

Bishop Henry and the preachers would see to it that I walked through fire and groveled in the dust, that there was no remaining shred of rebellion in me. They would hector me until I was witless, half-mad with stress. And I would submit, utterly, basely, to their satisfaction before they would restore my membership and lift the excommunication. I was trapped, completely at their mercy.

Even so, I was welcomed that first Sunday morning as we stood around outside before the service. People shook my hand and smiled. I walked inside and sat with my peers in my normal spot. Feeling a bit like a lamb walking to slaughter, I got up during the first song and followed the preachers to their Obrote, or conference, as I had done years before during baptismal classes. But this time I was the only one. There was no baptismal class. Just me. I followed the preachers into the side room and shut the door.

Outside the room, the congregation roared joyfully the ancient hymns of my childhood. I took a seat facing all the preachers. Quite a lineup that morning, including a few from the north district. Maybe they'd heard I was returning and had come over to join the action. Get their digs in. I sat silently. A brief moment passed. Bishop Henry cleared his throat.

This time, he addressed me directly. Broad, vacant bromides would flow soon enough, but first, the rules must be established. Bishop Henry opened with a short welcome. He was so glad—he claimed with a frozen smile—to see that I had changed my attitude and now was willing to seek redemption and forgiveness from God and the church. All the other preachers nodded in assent but remained silent. I said nothing. I wasn't expected to say anything.

Then Bishop Henry looked right at me. "To seek forgiveness from sin, one must first confess those sins," he intoned. "We now request that you confess all your specific sins, here to us in this room. As best you can remember."

So *that* was how it went. I didn't know. I'd never done this before. Now I was expected to speak. Directed to speak. To confess my sins. All the bad stuff I'd done. *Oh boy*. They had me. Did they ever have me. I sat in that somber room and looked at them. Faced them all. They leaned toward me, restrained but eager. It might have been my imagination in the stress of that moment, but their eyes seemed to shine hungrily. At least the eyes of some of them. Whether or not that actually was the case, one fact cannot be disputed. I was surrounded and alone.

This, then, is what the mad bishop of Ligonier had wrought by his rigid refusal to reinstate me in his church. It would have been so much easier to confess my sins to strangers. To preachers who knew little of my past, preachers who had seen it all before. Now, before these men, all of whom were quite familiar with my history, I was expected to confess the sins I had committed. To speak of them, recite them in minute detail. It was a harsh and bitter thing.

I swallowed. Stuttered a bit. And then, speaking in a halting monotone, pausing now and then as I tried to remember specifics, I told them all my sins, all the things I had done on my latest flight. All the bad stuff I'd done over the past year. How I had drunk. Got stoned. Run around with English women. All the things one did when one stepped outside the box. I didn't even bother to mention the obvious things like driving and owning a pickup truck. They already knew that. They wanted the juicier details, and I didn't let them down. Surprisingly, it didn't take that long. When I finished, Bishop Henry and all the preachers looked properly and officially grieved. Actually, they seemed a little stunned. I don't know what they were expecting.

After regaining his composure, Bishop Henry claimed to be very glad at my honesty. Then he proceeded to admonish me at some length. I'm sure his head was spinning from my long list of sins. After he wrapped up, the other preachers all spoke for a few minutes, also sternly admonishing me while simultaneously claiming to be overjoyed at my return and repentance. They didn't seem too joyous, but in that room, at that awkward moment, I was certainly willing to take their word for it.

And then I was dismissed to return to the congregation. I walked back into the crowded room, head held high. I would not cower before these people. The room echoed with the roars of slow tune singing, but all eyes were glued to me as I took my seat on a bench among my peers.

Usually, it takes about four weeks to be reinstated. Church is every two weeks, so that means you trail along behind the preachers twice. And then it's enough. Then there's a special ceremony at the end of the service after the nonmembers and children are dismissed, and the repentant sinner is officially welcomed back into the fold.

But four weeks was not long enough in my case. Not according to Bishop Henry. Because of the seriousness of my sins, it would take at least six weeks, maybe eight.

During that time, I stayed close to home and didn't socialize much. Officially, my family was required to shun me, which consisted mostly of not eating at the same table. When Mom prepared the meals, she set a plate for me on a little side table. We all dipped food from the same dishes and ate at the same time, a few feet apart. When the married children came home for supper during the week, we ate cafeteria style, again dipping Mom's delicious food from the same dishes. I always made sure to sit a bit apart on a side bench. In all other respects, I was treated as usual. We separated only when we ate. Which didn't make a whole lot of sense back then, and still doesn't. But that's the way it was.

I saw Sarah at least twice in informal settings. We talked. She was as beautiful as ever, except her face was drawn and sad. I felt sorry for her and for what I had done, but I still didn't regret it. We spoke, publicly and privately, from depths of pain that could not be expressed or even acknowledged.

I meandered up to Chuck's Café once in a while, but not often; too many eyes were watching my every step, too many people hoping I would stumble. Too much time at Chuck's would not be viewed as repentant behavior, so I dropped by only now and then. I told my old friends what was going on. They didn't understand, but they listened and sympathized. And slowly, I began to withdraw from them emotionally. I knew I could not hang around them often. It would remind me too much of all I was giving up.

Finally, after six long weeks, the glorious Sunday arrived when I would be "taken up," restored as a full member of the Bloomfield Amish church. I walked along behind the preachers that morning into the conference for the final time. Ever. After the usual admonitions, I was dismissed for the last time to return to the congregation.

I don't remember who preached that day. It might have been my brother Joseph. The hours dragged. I knew what was coming, and it would not be pretty. Finally, the service wound down, and the last song was sung. Bishop Henry announced where church service would be held in two weeks, and then he dismissed the congregation, requesting that all members remain seated for a few moments.

The youth who were not members got up and walked out,

as did all the children. I walked out, too, and stood uneasily just outside the house. Ten, maybe fifteen minutes passed. Inside, the preachers were announcing that in their opinion, I had shown the proper degree of repentance, and it was now time to reinstate me as a member. They requested counsel from all members. Anyone who objected could speak or forever hold his peace.

And then the deacon popped out of the house and looked around for me. I approached. "Come along," he said kindly. He walked back inside, and I followed close behind him, right up to the front, where everyone could see me. I sat on a bench before the bishop. The room was completely still.

Bishop Henry rose to his feet and addressed me. They had counseled with all members who were present, and no one had any objections. If my desire was still to be reinstated as I had expressed that morning in the Obrote conference, I should get down on my knees.

And for the second time in my life, I knelt before God and the Amish church. Bishop Henry recited a rote list of questions. I don't remember exactly what they were, but something to the effect that I had realized the error of my ways, confessed my sins, repented, and requested to rejoin the church as a full member. After each question, he paused. And after each question I answered yes.

It was an inverse version of my baptism. The somber stillness. The rote ceremony. The restrained joy of a lost sheep found. After the final question, Bishop Henry paused, then spoke. "Before we proceed further, we will pray. Will the congregation please stand?" And all rose to their feet. I remained on my knees.

Bishop Henry launched into a long, recited prayer, his voice rising and falling in a rhythmic flow. After the prayer ended, everyone was seated once again. Bishop Henry approached and stood before me. He extended his hand, and I reached out and grasped it.

"In the name of God and the church, I extend my hand," he intoned. "Arise." I stood. Before that room of witnesses, in the silence reflecting ancient ritual, we greeted each other with the holy kiss. I stood there, unmoving, as Bishop Henry kindly wished me well in the future and hoped that I would always remain true to the vows I had just spoken. Then it was over. I was restored as a full member. Bishop Henry motioned me to my seat, and I sat there as we were dismissed.

It's hard now to describe my feelings in that moment. I suppose I felt as lost as I ever had. But I smiled and shook the hands of those who came to wish me well. This would be my last Sunday in Bloomfield, Iowa, as a member of the Old Order Amish church.

And then the day ended, as all days must. I planned to leave the next week and head back to northern Indiana. Back to Phillip and Fannie and their large, empty home. Back to a new community for a fresh new start, where I would make my mark in life.

Before leaving, I sold my buggy, the Mullet model, still as good as new, with its shiny, black velvet interior. It had not been used much in my absence. I advertised it in the local *Penny Saver* at a hugely discounted price, and it sold the first day.

Before the next Sunday arrived, I shook the dust from Bloomfield. I never returned—as an Amish person.

32

I BOARDED THE TRAIN IN OTTUMWA and traveled back to Ligonier, where Phillip and Fannie welcomed me. They were solid, simple people, happy to do what they could to help.

And so began my time in northern Indiana. I settled in, landing a job at the Starcraft RV factory in Topeka. I would make it this time. I would *force* myself to make it. Too much was riding on this effort, including my own salvation.

It was not an easy road, settling in a strange land like that. Not being from the area, I found little social structure geared to my needs. Too old to run with the local youth and not really interested in the singings, I hung out with Phillip and his social circle, which I found to be daunting and ultimately very discouraging.

The northern Indiana Amish were good, steady people, just a bit different from anything I'd ever known. Actually, a lot different. They were entrenched in their own ways and their own habits, and none, as far as I could tell, had the slightest interest in the world outside the boundaries of their communities. Many were willfully ignorant and seemed determined to remain so.

But having traveled this far, I bravely soldiered on. I applied for membership in the Ligonier District. The mad bishop smiled grimly but kept his promise to accept me as a member of his church—even though it was clear he did not expect me to make it. To him, I was plainly a heathen, someone not to be trusted. I wouldn't last. He had sensed that from the moment he met me. Maybe that's why I disliked him so much. The man had me pegged from the start, and the truth was more than I could take, especially from someone like him. A spiteful, power-mad husk of a man.

As the weeks passed, then the months, I developed a daily routine. Went to work each day on my bicycle and rode the five miles home each night, in every kind of weather. The factory was my only social outlet, and I made a few friends there. Good guys. Decent guys. They were my age or younger, and all of them were married. But outside of work, we rarely socialized. They attempted to include me a few times, and I accepted now and then, but mostly, their social groups held little appeal. So I had a lot of time to kill on my own.

Around the farm, I helped Phillip and Fannie with their chores each night and chatted with them about their day and mine. It was all pretty idyllic.

And stifling.

I immersed myself in books. Each night I read and read in the flickering flame of the oil lamp in my bedroom.

And slowly, slowly, the truth seeped into my brain. It was not working. I had probably realized that fact long before admitting it to myself. I was stuck in a deadly dull routine. And there seemed no way it would ever improve. I simply could not do it. Could not fit in. The northern Indiana Amish were unassuming;

good-natured; and unlike me, utterly content within the confines of their community and their world.

I loved these people. They were the salt of the earth and would have done anything for me. They wanted me to make it, to succeed there. They wanted me as a part of their church and their community. I appreciated that then. I still do.

But we simply could not connect beyond a certain intellectual point. Not that they were stupid. They weren't. It's just that, well, their world was not mine. It was not like any I had ever known. And when we were together, bantering and talking, I sometimes felt as if I simply could not take it anymore. I couldn't take one more breathless tale of whose cow broke through the fence and got out on the road. Who ran his bicycle into the ditch and broke his leg. Whose horse ran away and crashed the buggy into a car. Not one more story of who said what and who did what and wasn't it all just awful?

In time, their perceived faults accumulated in my mind and rankled me deeply. I recoiled instinctively from the provincial banality of my surroundings. And, sadly, I even recoiled from my good-hearted friends. I began to see them as uncouth and couldn't stand their hard, mirthless laughter at some silly, utterly senseless joke. Their smug, deliberate ignorance.

And from there, it was only a matter of time until I realized it was all in vain. All my efforts. All my plans. Utter failures. These kind, simple people were not my people and would never be. The mad bishop had been right. I could not make it here. I would not make it here. I could not stay.

I had exerted so much effort and invested so much time in this last attempt. Always, I really had believed that in some vague and distant future, everything would work out. Always I had faith there would be rest from the weary road just ahead. A peaceful place of green pastures, where I would see and be satisfied and content to live in quietness and peace as an Amish man.

But that vague and distant future, where it would all work out, had arrived. And it wasn't working out. The whole thing had been a figment of my mind, of my hopes, of my imagination. It had been long and arduous, this latest journey of return. So much time. So many miles. And now it was crumpling. All that effort, for nothing.

I could no longer ignore the brutal truth of my circumstances. And dull panic stirred inside me, because I knew that if I left this time, there would be no return. This time would be the last time. This time, I would be admitting to all the world that I was lost, with no hope of ever attaining salvation. This time, it would be over.

Forever.

As the realization set in, I sank into quiet, desperate despair. I became depressed, silent, and brooding, with no one in whom to confide. Phillip and Fannie were kind and supportive, but there was no way they would understand or comprehend what I was going through. I knew that if I tried to talk to them, they would simply spout the usual clichés: "Just decide to do what's right, and then do it."

But that's what I had been trying to do, all these many months, these many miles. Doing what was right, or what I believed was right. It wasn't working. I was, in fact, failing spectacularly. There was no sense in continuing. No sense in constantly knocking my head against the wall. And so I remained silent, confided in no one, and slipped ever deeper into that mental trench of darkness from which I could see no way out.

And then, sometime during the darkness of those desperate days, it came to me. A sliver of light, an idea. I don't know how or from where. Although I'd been taught all my life to pray, I never did much, because I never saw that it did any good. Not for those around me, at least. Every day the Amish launched some of the most beautifully written prayers out there. It was a formal thing, praying. Approach God, read some poetic lines from a little black book, and then get up and go about your day, secure in the knowledge that you had done your duty, that you would be protected. In church, of course, every single syllable in every prayer was scripted, read from a book or memorized, word for word. That's all I knew about praying. All I had ever seen.

Normally, I wouldn't have considered praying, not for a second. It would never have crossed my mind. Even if it had, I would have shrugged it off. But this was not a normal time.

I decided that I could simply talk to God. Ask for his help. Not by reading from a little black book, but by talking to him, man to man. Or man to God. Whatever.

I thought about it. I figured it wouldn't work. But, hey, it couldn't hurt to try. What was there to lose? So one day I did. I spoke to God. Informally. I don't remember my specific words, only that I prayed. I had no desire to remain Amish. In my mind, I equated that with having no desire to do what was right.

My request was a simple, desperate plea: *God, I don't expect you to hear me. I mean, why would you? But if you do hear, give me the desire to do what's right. I don't have even that much.*

And that was it. Nothing profound. No *Amen*, even. No flash of enlightenment struck me. I still felt exactly the same and trudged on through the dreariness of everyday life, forgetting even that I had prayed. I had little hope—actually none—that my prayer would be heard, much less answered. God didn't have time for wicked people like me. Not after all I had done. Not after so deliberately, so frequently, turning my back on everything I had been taught from childhood. Most likely I had blasphemed the Holy Spirit, which meant there was no hope for me. Ever.

I was lost. And I knew I was lost.

33

HE WALKED INTO MY LIFE less than a month later, unexpectedly and abruptly, as I was strolling along the sidewalk in the small town of Topeka after work. I didn't pay any attention to him as he approached. Topeka swarmed with Amish people, from morning until night. Bearded men of every type. Women bundled in bonnets and shawls, lugging squalling babies. And Amish children everywhere. They were total strangers to me, except for the few I had gotten to know at work and in church. Mostly, I paid them no mind. And mostly, they ignored me.

But this man glanced at me sharply and then walked straight toward me. He was tall and thin as a rail. He was obviously married, with a long black beard, and he had finely honed, sensitive features. The ubiquitous black felt hat perched on his head, covering a full head of straight-hanging hair. Closer, closer we walked toward each other. His piercing gaze never left my face. I would have brushed past him and continued on my way, but he stopped and smiled, looking right at me. So I stopped too. *Who was this wacko, and what did he want?*

"Hello. You must be a stranger in these parts." He smiled, extending his hand.

Sure a friendly chap, whoever he was. I smiled back and grasped his hand. "I am."

"I'm Sam Johnson," he said. "Who are you?"

Johnson. Johnson. Strange name, for an Amish man. "Ira Wagler," I replied. I waited for the inevitable flash of recognition. *Wagler. Wagler.* And sure enough, it came.

"Wagler?" he exclaimed. "Not related to David Wagler? Are you his son?"

I admitted that I was, though rather sheepishly.

He chuckled. "Well, well. Imagine that, meeting the son of that famous man on the streets of Topeka." And somehow, strangely, I was instantly at ease and chuckled back at him.

Sam was different. I sensed that right off. He was sharp and intelligent, asking keen, incisive questions. From anyone else, it would have been offensive. But somehow, from him, the questions were okay. He was curious, and that was fine. I was intrigued. We stood there on the sidewalk in Topeka, Indiana, on that sunny fall afternoon and talked comfortably, like old friends. Like we'd known each other our whole lives.

His story flowed freely from him. He had not been born or raised Amish. As a young single man, he had joined from the outside—learned the language, joined the church, married, and had a family.

It is almost impossible to pull off something like that, to join the Amish from outside society. A lot of people think they want to, even believe they will, until they try it. Over the years, hundreds have made the attempt, but probably fewer than a dozen or two have actually pulled it off. Once they get inside the culture, the romance wears off in a week or two. The harsh, plain lifestyle. The endless hours of labor, from dawn to dusk and beyond. And even if they clear those hurdles somehow, the language barrier nails them. You gotta want it, really want it, to hang in there. It's an almost impossible accomplishment, especially long term.

I stood there and gaped openly at him as he told me his tale. "How could you do something like that?" "What in the world possessed you to even want to?" I actually asked those questions the first time I met him. And a whole lot more. And I didn't even know the man. I was entranced, almost mesmerized by our conversation. It was like an oasis, out here in the middle of this barren desert in which I was dying of thirst.

He sensed my eager, hungry mind, and we stood there talking as time passed. First minutes, then an hour. Suddenly then, he pulled back, startled, and glanced at his pocket watch. He must be getting on home. His wife was expecting him, and he was already running way late.

I wasn't ready to let him go just yet. "When can we talk again?" I asked.

He seemed as excited as I was. "We can meet again, here in town, after work. Soon, very soon. I'll check with my wife, so we can talk longer," he answered.

As we parted, he spoke words that jolted me: "It's not by chance we met this afternoon."

I could only nod. I biked home in a daze. Finally, a man who understood me. A man with whom I could actually communicate. It seemed like a miracle.

That night, over supper, I told Phillip and Fannie about the man I'd met. Who in the world was he? Where did he come from? They knew him. Of course they did. Everyone, it turned out, knew Sam Johnson. Phillip and his wife seemed excited that I had met someone who had impressed me so deeply.

In the weeks that followed, Sam and I met regularly. Usually in town. And our friendship grew. He invited me to his house for supper one evening. I met his smiling, beautiful wife, Ellen, and his two rambunctious young sons. It was a lovely little household, and something stirred inside me, seeing him with his family. He had it all, it seemed. Why couldn't something like that be mine as well?

It could have been, of course, with Sarah, back in Bloomfield. But somehow, it didn't seem the same, what he had and what I could have had.

Within a month, we were fast friends. Best friends. I learned to trust him as I had trusted no one in my life before.

He listened a lot and spoke a lot. He challenged me, both intellectually and mentally. When I grumbled about the Amish, their simplemindedness and their shallow uncouthness, he heard me. And he agreed, to a point. But he always came back with a question.

"If it's so bad, why don't you stay and make it better? We desperately need people like you in the Amish church. You are a born leader. You could tremendously influence the culture and the church in your lifetime."

And his perspective always left me silent, groping for a comeback. I came back a time or two. "You don't understand, don't realize the bad things I've done. You don't know where I've been. And besides, I don't know if I even believe in God. What use can the Amish possibly have for a man like me?"

Even those words, anathema to any ordinary Amish man, did not shock him.

And in time, I told him who I was. Of how I was so lost and so afraid. Of how I was approaching the end here in this area. Of the mad bishop of Ligonier and how I couldn't take it anymore. I told him of my past, sparing no details. What I'd done, how I'd left home again and again. The people I had hurt, so senselessly and so deeply. I told him of Sarah and of all the guilt associated with that terrible experience. Haltingly, brokenly, I let the words flow from me. I left out nothing. Spared no details.

"You have done nothing that cannot be forgiven," he answered after I finished. "Nothing. I don't care what you've done. There is a place where you can let it all go, let it rest, and return to life. Trust me on this."

And so it went, back and forth, for weeks. We talked of many other things too. My irritation at the Amish in general, my disconnection with the culture, and of his own journey to where he was. It seemed strange, and I told him so. We were traveling in opposite directions. Born of English blood, he was more Amish than the Amish. And I, born of the purest Amish bloodlines, was heading away, out into the world from which he had come. And yet somehow, we had met on our journeys and connected so strongly. Strange, indeed.

I absorbed all the things he said about forgiveness and about new life. And gradually, his words began to penetrate my mind. He explained that there was no human penance for my sins. No way I could ever atone for all the things I had done. But, Sam reminded me again and again, there was someone else who *could* atone. Who could wipe the past away and give new life. Heal all the wounds—my own and those I had inflicted on so many others through the years. It seemed impossible that it could be true. But I listened, and I desperately wanted to believe him.

He never pressured me. Never told me to "just decide to do what's right." Or "to just straighten up and settle down." I guess that's because he wasn't raised Amish. He didn't buy into those trite, simplistic lines. He was simply my friend. Quietly there, just there, regardless of who I was or what I had done.

And gradually, gently, the man calmed my spirit and gave me

hope. He led me to realize that my rough and rowdy past could be forgiven. That all the pain and all the wounds could be healed. That there was real hope and a new life for me, should I choose to take it. Accept it. Live it.

Gradually, too, the struggles and doubts that had haunted me since my early teens began to fade. I could do this. I could change. I could choose to believe. I thought it through for a long time. Days. Then weeks. It could be true. It must be true.

And then one day, the moment arrived. I would do it. See what happened. I'm not sure what motivated me. Exhaustion, I guess. That, and a tiny seed of faith that had somehow sprouted from somewhere. That day, that afternoon, I spoke to God again. Informally again. Not in despair this time, but as a man who dared to hope. A man who wanted to do what was right. From his heart.

My first desperate prayer, a few months back, had been heard and answered.

By quietly showing me Christ's love, my friend had led me to the Source of that love. For the first time, I truly grasped that Christ had died for me—suffered, bled, and died—and that I could be his through faith. I was amazed at how simple it really was. Why had it always seemed so hard, so impossible before?

I waited, then, for the light. Would it be in vain, like before? Like when I was baptized and felt nothing? Like when I returned to the Amish church, walked the gauntlet, and felt nothing? Would this end up the same? I waited. And it came. Almost immediately, a huge load of despair and anguish was lifted from me, replaced with a deep, quiet sense of joy and an internal peace beyond anything I had ever known. I couldn't believe it. This could not be happening. Not to me. But it was.

And so, alone in my room that day on my cousin's farm in Ligonier, Indiana, I reached the end of a long and tortured road, a road that had meandered through all the days and weeks and years of adulthood. A weary road of almost ten years. The end of my frenzied running from I knew not what to I knew not where. It all ended there, with a simple request for new birth and new life.

He who gives life to the lifeless gave life to me. I wanted to tell someone. Not shout, but at least express it somehow. But I couldn't. Not among the Amish. They would view my experience with grave suspicion. The mad bishop would launch an inquisition for sure, which would not be pretty. But it wouldn't be just him; others would look askance as well. Quiet and reserved, the Amish are not given to emotional testimonies about salvation.

I couldn't wait, though, to tell Sam the next time we met. It would be okay. He would understand. And when I told him, he didn't seem too surprised. He smiled quietly, and tears suddenly filled his eyes. "Welcome, brother," was all he said.

And for me, it was like a new day had dawned. For the first time as an adult, I faced the future without fear. Not that the future was clear, because it wasn't. And not that there weren't a lot of issues to deal with, because there were. But somehow, I relaxed. I let go of all the emotional baggage that had burdened me for so long. Just released it. And it's not that it disappeared magically, because it didn't. It lurked out there on the edges of my consciousness like a ghost. It was still frightening sometimes, but it didn't get to me. I knew and held on to the truth. I was now a child of God. Nothing could take that from me. Not the sins of my past. Not the pain of all those vivid memories. Not the fear of death or dying. Nothing.

34

SAM HAD ALWAYS STRONGLY ENCOURAGED ME to value and embrace my Amish heritage. That's where he was, firmly established in the culture he had adopted as his own. He longed for me to be there and to share it with him. Together, he believed, we could go far. But I was dubious. Why would I stay with these simple people? Sure, they held on to a lot of the old ways. Some things were good. And some of their traditions, too, were okay in my mind. But their studied, deliberate ignorance still rankled and bothered me—a lot. And I confronted Sam over and over again. Why? Why would I stay?

Always, he had the same response. "You are your father's son," he said. "Gifted, like he is. Like he was all his life. Your dad is getting along in years. The Amish will need someone to take his place. Someone to write, to define and explain their faith. Their lifestyle. Defend it. You have a strong personality. Leadership qualities. So why not you?"

I had no comeback for that. And after my conversion experience, that suddenly didn't seem that important anymore. In the new, settled calmness of life, I decided to hang around for a while. See what happened. Come what may, I could take it. I even managed to dredge up a few good vibes for the mad bishop. Well, maybe that's going too far. I didn't have good vibes, but my intense hostility toward the man diminished miraculously, mostly because I removed myself from his presence.

Late in the fall of that year, I moved out of his district and northwest, into the Goshen area. A nice older Amish couple, Sam's friends, had an empty house on a small lot with an old dilapidated barn. They wanted someone to live there and maintain it. On Sam's recommendation, they offered it to me for low rent. So I moved to a new district.

In the larger Amish communities, the rules can vary greatly from district to district. In one, you might be allowed power lawn mowers, rubber rims on your buggy wheels, and other progressive things. In another, you might be allowed only hand-powered push mowers, steel-rimmed buggy wheels, and so forth. A bishop's policies can drastically affect the value of real estate in his district. The more progressive the bishop, the higher the value of land and homes, because everyone wants to live there. Not surprisingly, real estate values in the mad bishop's district ranked way down there, among the lowest in all of northern Indiana. You could almost buy a farm there for the price of a simple house and lot in the northern districts.

Goshen was among the most progressive Amish areas in northern Indiana. A land of Canaan and the focus of the wishful gaze of many longing eyes from the southern districts. I was happy to shake the Ligonier dust from my feet and move to a land free of harsh, strange people like the mad bishop. A land of milk and honey. Goshen.

I never saw the mad bishop again. I never missed him, either.

• • •

I settled into my new home, a rather ramshackle place, but livable. Batching it, alone, for the first time in my life. Mostly, I liked it. An English coworker from Goshen picked me up each morning for the ride to the factory in Topeka, as it was too far to bike, and I paid him a few bucks every week in return. Soon, I decided to go buggy shopping. I found a nice rig with rubber-tired rims, which were fully allowed in my new progressive church. I also bought a plump little mare, not too wild and fully road trained. I was set.

My Goshen Amish neighbors all welcomed me. They stopped by, introduced themselves, and invited me over for supper. They included me in their lives as best they knew how.

An elderly Amish widow lived alone next door, a few hundred feet away. Barbara was suspicious when I first showed up at her doorstep, but she warmed up immediately after we had chatted a bit. Might she have an old copy of *The Budget* I could borrow? I wanted to catch up on the news and Dad's latest letters. Her crinkled face lit up. Oh, yes, she did. After that, it became a weekly tradition. I stopped by to read the latest copy, sitting at her kitchen table, while she fussed and mothered me. Smiling, she served coffee and cookies while filling me in on the latest local gossip. Much of the time I had no idea what she was talking about, but I smiled politely and listened, commenting now and then where I could. We laughed a lot together. Lonely since her husband's death a few years before, she eagerly anticipated my visits. In some small way, we each filled a void in the other's life. I had no family in the area. Widowed and childless, she was alone. We quickly became fast friends.

It was one of the most idyllic periods of my life as an Amish person, outside of childhood. Settled and calm, I absorbed and lived each day. I enjoyed life and laughed again. Not the hard, desperate laughter of the past, but the true thing, laughter from the heart, deep and real. I still saw Sam regularly, and we hung out as much as possible. He beamed at the new me and checked now and then to make sure I was still doing okay in my newfound faith. I was.

Holed up in my bachelor home, with little social life, I buried myself in books. By then I had accumulated quite an impressive library of my own. Each evening, after a meager supper of soup and sandwich, I lit the kerosene lantern and read into the late hours of the night, working my way through Will Durant's *The Story of Civilization* and random chunks and chapters from dozens of other books. My mind was hungry, and I fed it. And each night, long after the dim lights died in the houses of my Amish neighbors, I sat there, absorbing and devouring knowledge from those pages.

But it was not good to be alone so much. A man needs people around him, some sort of structural support. My friends tried to provide what support they could, but they all had friends and families of their own.

A single guy with no connections will quickly fall through the cracks, as I did. But to be honest, I didn't really want to hang around that much with most of the people anyway. Sam and the widow Barbara, those two relationships I cherished. The others I could take or leave. Mostly, I left them, preferring my own company to theirs.

The long and lonely evening hours got to me eventually. And something stirred in me that winter, the winter of my discontent. Not the old frantic discontent of the past, but a yearning deep inside to be free. Free of the cultural chains that bound me. Free of this confining Amish life. And this time, as the deep longings stirred within, I realized for the first time in my life that I *could* leave.

Leave and not be lost.

It took awhile, to get my mind around a thing like that. To

examine it, test it, and really grasp it without fear. To face it, accept it. The box of Amish life and culture might provide some protection, but it could never bring salvation.

And once I really truly grasped that fact, it was only a matter of time until the course of my future changed forever.

* * *

I didn't just pack up and leave the next day, or disappear, with no word to those around me. I didn't even consider such a course. I pondered the issue for days, weeks. Did I really, really want to give it all up? I had invested a tremendous amount of time and effort to reach this place, both my physical surroundings and the place of peace in my mind and heart. I had experienced a miraculous spiritual rebirth here in this area, as an Amish person.

And always, Sam's words echoed in my head: *Why not stay? Why not take on your father's work? The Amish need people like you. Why not you?*

In those long evening hours alone in that house that winter, I pondered. Thought it through. Maybe Sam was right. Maybe, just maybe, I should stay. Be the man I could be among the Amish. The man Sam thought I should be.

I thought, too, of my parents back in Bloomfield. How disappointed they would be, especially Mom. For years, she had ridden the emotional seesaw, shifting back and forth between sadness and joy, sadness and joy, and if I left, sadness. Again. Even so, I realized the choice would have to be mine. Not their choice, and not Sam's.

But my choice, for my life.

Then came spring, and new life sprouted on the land. And in the end, I could not find it in my heart to stay. I would not take up my father's mantle.

Sam had sensed the change in me that winter. I had shared with him honestly the path I was considering, and he could feel it coming. He knew that I would not stay. I saw the hurt in his eyes and the deep sense of disappointment and loss. And I saw, too, that he could not quite deal with it.

In those final weeks and days, an awkward tension sprouted between us. I wanted so much for him to see and understand my newfound freedom. To recognize that what I had was real. I wanted him to bless my life and to bless me. He deeply longed for me to stay and be the person he knew I could be in the Amish church, to fulfill his vision and his dream for me. To be the person he knew I could be.

And he may have been right. I might have been that person.

But there was one problem. That was not the person I wanted to be. Sam's vision and his dreams were not mine. I wanted to speak to him, to tell him the truth, but I could not break through the final wall of pain and silence that separated us.

Quietly then, I made my plans. I called my friends in Daviess. My brother Nathan had recently moved to Pennsylvania. So I called the Wagler family, Dean and his brothers, and asked if someone could come up and get me. Of course they would. They didn't ask a lot of questions. One of the brothers would be dispatched. We settled on a date.

In calmness, then, I wrapped up my affairs in Goshen. I quit my job at the factory, sold my horse and buggy, and packed up my stuff. To my curious neighbors, I said only that I was moving south. Not back to Ligonier and the mad bishop, but way south, to Daviess, the land of my fathers. They smiled kindly, as if they understood. It probably made more sense to them than the fact that I, a stranger with no family in the area, had tried to settle among them.

Only to the widow Barbara was I honest. I told her my plans, and where I was going, that I was leaving the Amish and joining a Mennonite church in Daviess. She was sad, but only because I was leaving and because I wouldn't come around anymore to read *The Budget* and drink her coffee. Of all my friends in northern Indiana, she would miss me the most. I stopped by as often as I could during those last few days.

And then the day arrived. I got up early and walked down the road to say good-bye to Barbara, my surrogate mother. In the final moments, she wept quietly, grasped my arm, then hugged me tight. For a minute or so, she could not speak. But then she smiled through her tears.

"Go," she said. "Go in peace, and go with God. Stop in and see me when you are in the area."

"I will," I promised. And we stood there in heavy silence. There was nothing more to say. We knew, both of us, that this might be the last time we saw each other. She was elderly, in her seventies, and might not survive many more years. We both knew full well that I would most likely never come around again.

Dean's younger brother, Nate, arrived a short time later, and we quickly loaded my few belongings in his van. I walked through the house one last time, checking for any misplaced items, locked the door, placed the key under the mat outside, got into the van, and we were off.

We pulled onto the road and passed the widow Barbara's house. I saw her wrinkled face clearly, watching through the glass. She waved. I waved back.

I never said good-bye to Sam. Things between us were tense, really tense, by then. Our hearts were hardened toward each other. And so even this departure, so different from all the others in my past, was tinged with sadness and regret.

But my face was set to the south, to a new beginning. My heart was calm. My soul content. Behind us, the Amish settlement of northern Indiana receded in the distance as, in time, it would recede into the mists of the memories of my past.

I was leaving the Amish. Again. There was no plan, long term, except perhaps in some vague, undefined sense. But I was quietly confident it would all work out. Tomorrow. Next week. Next year. In five years. And beyond.

For the first time, I was not running in frantic despair into some wild and dangerous horizon. For the first time, I was leaving with a clear mind, quietly focused on faith, not fear. For the first time, I was leaving behind all the baggage, all the tortured, broken dreams, all the pain of so much loss and heartbreak.

For the first time, I was focused on an unknown future. Whatever it held, it would be okay. I would be okay. This I knew in my heart. I felt it deeply. Calmly.

And this time I knew there would be no return.

EPILOGUE

MORE THAN TWO DECADES HAVE PASSED since the morning of my final departure from Goshen, Indiana, and the last vestiges of my Amish past. I could not have known that day of the many and tremendously varied experiences that awaited me. It's been a great, grand journey, unique in so many ways. Exhilarating at times, and frightening at others. Here and there the road has been rough, but always vastly exciting and mostly fulfilling.

I have never looked back. Except to reminisce, remember, and reflect. On how it was. And how it went.

The good things. And the bad.

Despite harboring some resentment at the Amish in general for a number of years, I have come to terms with the aftermath of that hard and desperate journey and the bitter turmoil of nearly a decade of wasted years. Would I wish such a journey, at such steep cost, on anyone, ever? Of course not. But had I not traveled that long and troubled road, I would not be the man I am today.

Sadly, after I made the choice to leave, my good friend Sam chose to turn his face from me in sorrow. Soon after my departure, I attempted to reach out to him once or twice, but my olive branch was ignored, rejected by his silence. After that, I gave up and let it go. We have not seen each other, or spoken face-to-face, in more than twenty years. But he was and is still one of the most important people I have ever encountered. When the chips were down, he did not hesitate but waded into the darkness to lead a lost soul to the Light.

He will always be my friend. Perhaps one day we'll meet again as brothers.

In the years that have passed since I last saw him, I have tried to do to others as he did to me. Meet people where they are. As they are. To reflect Christ's love, without judgment, in the messy details of everyday life.

And it's not as if my own life hasn't been messy at times during those years. It has been, now and then, sometimes brutally so. Mostly as a result of my own choices.

But God is who he is. Forever. Unchanging. And always there, even when he doesn't seem to be. This I have learned. And this I know. Ultimately, I rest in that knowledge.

And if my readers glean only one thing from my story, I hope that's it. That God is there, even when he seems far away.

Today, I reside in a quiet place. A place of calmness and rest and of acceptance of who I am. A place of gratitude for the miracle of life in each new day.

And even though they no longer claim me as one of their own, I deeply respect the people connected to me by blood or background—the Amish. Their culture and their faith. With all their flaws. And all their strengths. They are still a part of me and will always be. Even so, I would never dream of returning.

Ever.

I have no regrets for the road I chose. And I rarely wonder how life would have been on the road not taken.

ABOUT THE AUTHOR

IRA WAGLER was born in the small Old Order Amish community of Aylmer, Ontario, Canada. At seventeen, frustrated by the rules and restrictions of Amish life, Ira got up at 2:00 a.m., packed his duffel bag, left a note under his pillow, and walked away. Over the course of the next five years, Ira would return home and leave again numerous times, torn between the ingrained message that abandoning one's Amish heritage results in eternal damnation, and the freedom and possibilities offered by the English world.

At age twenty-six, Ira left the Amish for good. He is currently general manager of Graber Supply, LLC, and Pole Building Company in Lancaster County, Pennsylvania.